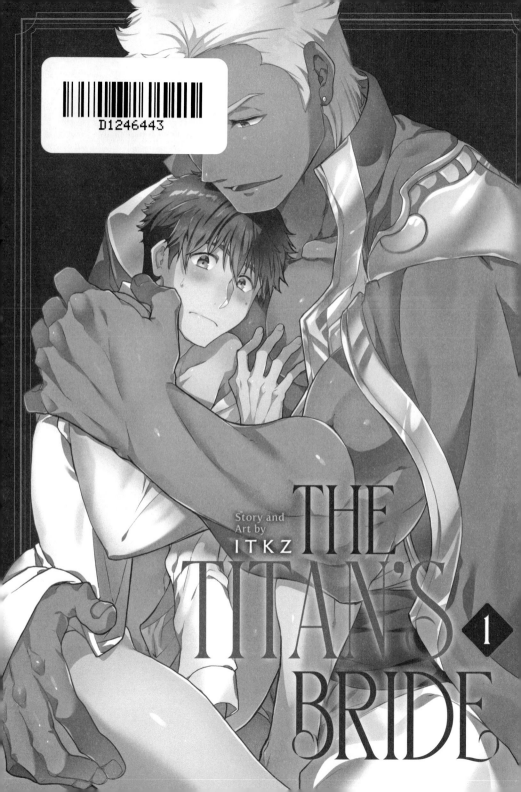

Story and
Art by
ITKZ

THE
TITAN'S
BRIDE

1

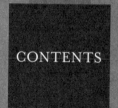

CONTENTS

Chapter 1   003

Chapter 2   027

Chapter 3   053

Chapter 4   079

Chapter 5   105

Chapter 6   131

Bonus Chapter   157

YOUR SMALL, DAINTY NECK...
HUFF!
HUFF!
WRISTS SO THIN THEY COULD SNAP...
NEVER IN MY LIFE HAVE I KNOWN A CREATURE ...
AS DELICATE AS YOU.
CREAK
KLAK
LOOM...
EEP ?!
I-IF YOU STICK THAT THING IN ME, I'LL...
FLINCH
Chapter 1

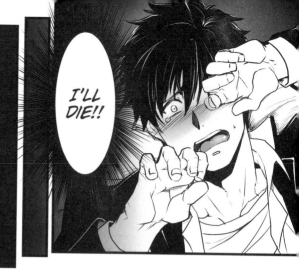

I'LL DIE!!

GREAT PRACTICE TODAY!

CAN'T BELIEVE THAT WAS MY LAST PRACTICE...

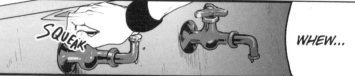

SQUEAK

WHEW...

MIZUKI-SENPAI!

TEP TEP TEP

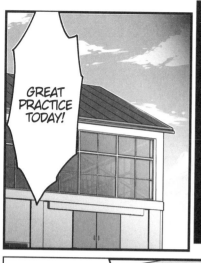

PHEW—

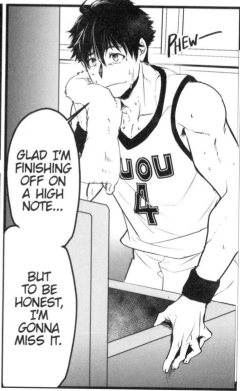

GLAD I'M FINISHING OFF ON A HIGH NOTE...

BUT TO BE HONEST, I'M GONNA MISS IT.

WE WANTED TO THANK YOU FOR YOUR THREE YEARS ON THE TEAM...

SO HERE! THIS IS FROM ALL OF US!

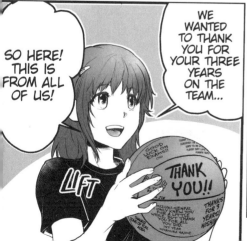

THANK YOU!!

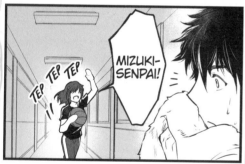

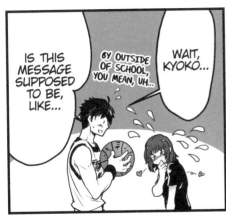

IS THIS MESSAGE SUPPOSED TO BE, LIKE...

BY OUTSIDE OF SCHOOL, YOU MEAN, UH...

WAIT, KYOKO...

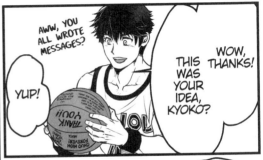

AWW, YOU ALL WROTE MESSAGES?

YUP!

WOW, THANKS! THIS WAS YOUR IDEA, KYOKO?

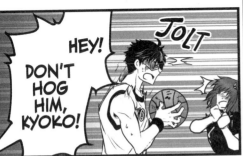

HEY!

JOLT

DON'T HOG HIM, KYOKO!

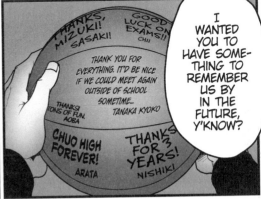

THANKS, MIZUKI!! SASAKI!!

GOOD LUCK ON EXAMS!! CHII

THANK YOU FOR EVERYTHING. IT'D BE NICE IF WE COULD MEET AGAIN OUTSIDE OF SCHOOL SOMETIME... TANAKA KYOKO

THANKS! TONS OF FUN. AOBA

CHUO HIGH FOREVER! ARATA

THANKS FOR 3 YEARS! NISHIKI

I WANTED YOU TO HAVE SOME- THING TO REMEMBER US BY IN THE FUTURE, Y'KNOW?

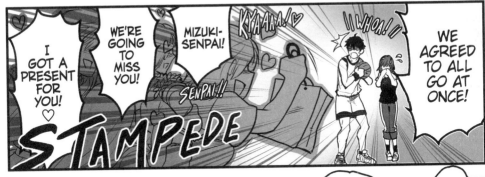

I GOT A PRESENT FOR YOU! ♡

WE'RE GOING TO MISS YOU!

MIZUKI- SENPAI!

KYAAAA! ♡

SENPAI!!

STAMPEDE

!!WHOA!!

WE AGREED TO ALL GO AT ONCE!

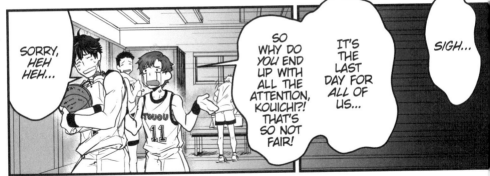

SORRY, HEH HEH...

SO WHY DO YOU END UP WITH ALL THE ATTENTION, KOUICHI?! THAT'S SO NOT FAIR!

IT'S THE LAST DAY FOR ALL OF US...

SIGH...

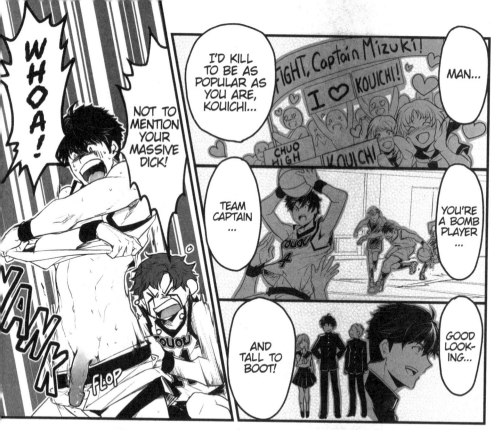

WHOA!

NOT TO MENTION YOUR MASSIVE DICK!

YANK

FLOP

I'D KILL TO BE AS POPULAR AS YOU ARE, KOUICHI...

FIGHT, Captain Mizuki! I ♥ KOUICHI! CHUO HIGH KOUICHI

MAN...

TEAM CAPTAIN...

YOU'RE A BOMB PLAYER...

AND TALL TO BOOT!

GOOD LOOK-ING...

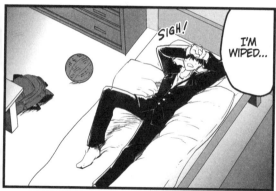

GET OFF ME, YOU DUMBASS!

THUD HA HA HA HA!

LET GO, DAMMIT! DRAG DRAG DRAG WAAAAH!!

YOU GOTTA SHARE! JUST ONE THING! YOUR BUDDY'S DYING OVER HERE!

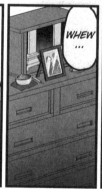

SIGH!

I'M WIPED...

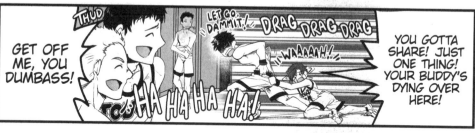

WHEW...

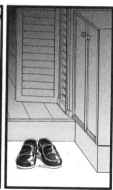

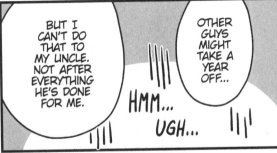

BUT I CAN'T DO THAT TO MY UNCLE. NOT AFTER EVERYTHING HE'S DONE FOR ME.

OTHER GUYS MIGHT TAKE A YEAR OFF...

HMM... UGH...

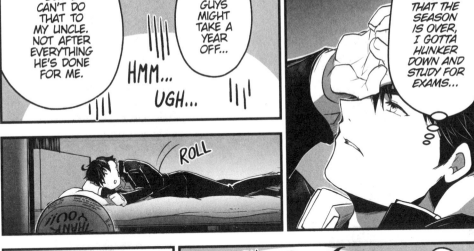

NOW THAT THE SEASON IS OVER, I GOTTA HUNKER DOWN AND STUDY FOR EXAMS...

ROLL

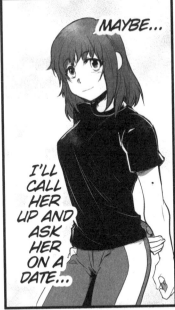

MAYBE...

I'LL CALL HER UP AND ASK HER ON A DATE...

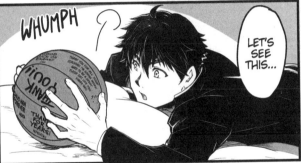

WHUMPH

LET'S SEE THIS...

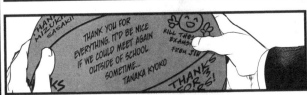

THANK YOU FOR EVERYTHING. IT'D BE NICE IF WE COULD MEET AGAIN OUTSIDE OF SCHOOL SOMETIME...
TANAKA KYOKO

KILL THOSE EXAMS

FROM JIN

THANKS FOR...!

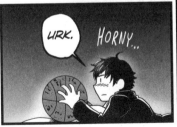

URK. HORNY...

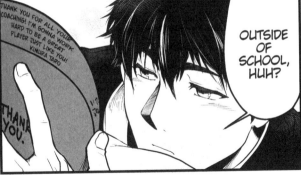

THANK YOU FOR ALL YOUR COACHING! I'M GONNA WORK HARD TO BE A GREAT PLAYER JUST LIKE YOU!
KIMURA TARO

THANK YOU.

OUTSIDE OF SCHOOL, HUH?

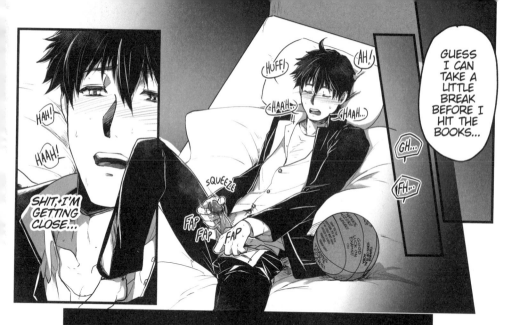

GUESS I CAN TAKE A LITTLE BREAK BEFORE I HIT THE BOOKS...

HAH! HAH!

HUFF! AH! HAAH... HAAH... HAAH...

GH... FH...

SHIT, I'M GETTING CLOSE...

SQUEEZE

FAP FAP FAP

I'VE FOUND YOU...

DID... SOMEONE SAY SOME-THING...?

? HFF! HFF!

...?

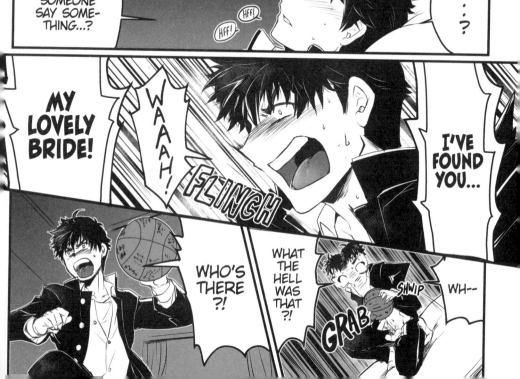

MY LOVELY BRIDE!

WAAAH!

FLINCH

I'VE FOUND YOU...

WHO'S THERE?!

WHAT THE HELL WAS THAT?!

WH--

GRAB

SHWIP

I'VE FOUND YOU!
?!
WHOA!!
IT'S TOO BRIGHT!
FLASH
MURMUR MURMUR MURMUR
IS THAT... TALKING?
MURMUR
TREMBLE
MURMUR
THANK YOU!!
MURMUR MURMUR
PEEK
WHAT THE HELL IS...
THANK YOU!!
HAPPE--

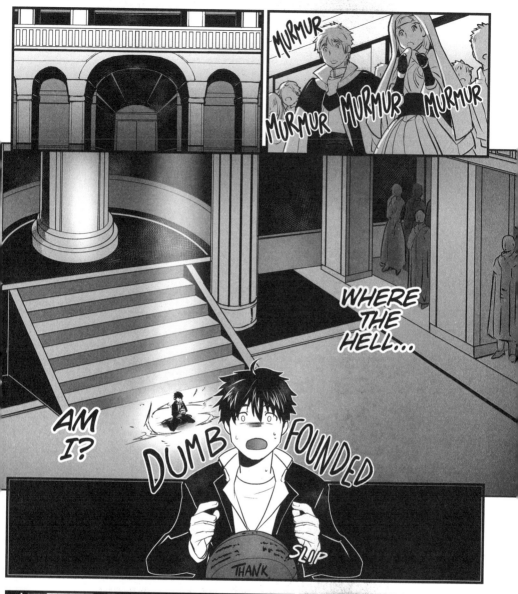

MURMUR

MURMUR MURMUR MURMUR

WHERE THE HELL...

AM I?

DUMB FOUNDED

SLIP

THANK

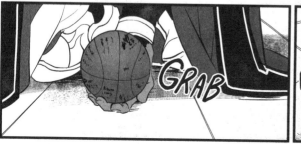

GRAB

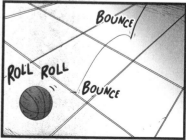

BOUNCE

ROLL ROLL

BOUNCE

HE'S...
HE'S HUGE!
AND...A FOREIGNER?
WE FINALLY MEET.

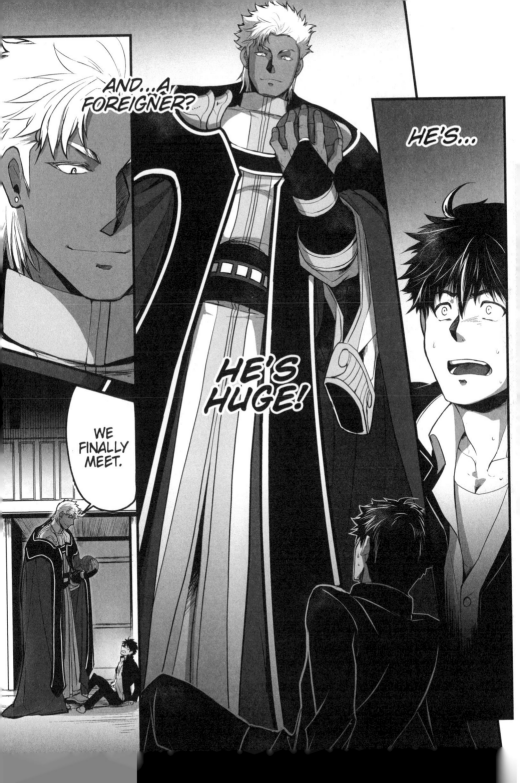

YOU ARE MY FATED PARTNER ...
GRASP
HEH HEH!
NEVER HAVE I ENCOUNTERED SOMEONE SO SMALL AND SWEET.
YOU'RE NOT UNLIKE A DELICIOUS, JUICY FRUIT.
POKE
ACK!
I FORGOT ABOUT THAT!
COME, NOW!
WHOA, HOLD ON!
THE RITUAL WAS A GRAND SUCCESS!
FLUTTER
EEK!
I'VE FOUND MY BRIDE!
SCOOP
A HALF-LING!
WHOOOOOA!!
THE PRINCE HAS SUMMONED A HALFLING!

WHO THE HELL ARE THEY...?

THE GIANT MAN THAT SCOOPED ME UP...

THEY'RE ALL HUGE!

CHEER

THE PRINCE'S BRIDE-TO-B IS A HALFLING!

CROWD

CLAMOR

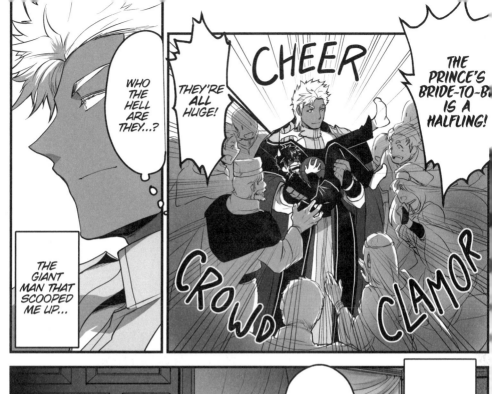

HEY, SO, UH, WHERE AM I?

AND WHO ARE YOU?

AND DEPOSITED ME ONTO A BED LIKE THIS SORT OF THING HAPPENED EVERY DAY.

BROUGHT ME TO A LUXURIOUS ROOM...

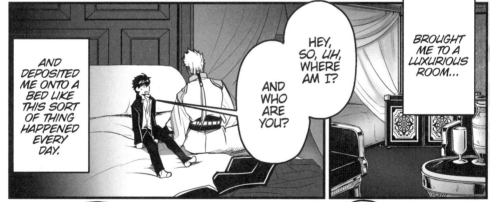

I AM THE CROWN PRINCE OF TILDANT, KINGDOM OF TITANS...

AND MY NAME IS CAIUS.

IT EXISTS IN A TIME AND PLACE FAR BEYOND YOUR OWN.

THIS LAND IS CALLED EUSTIL.

AND THAT WAS JUST THE BEGINNING OF THIS UNBELIEVABLE TALE.

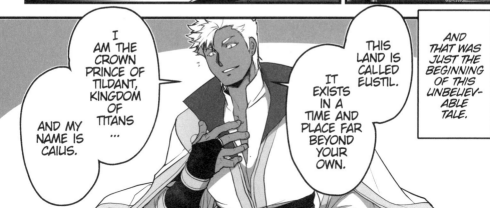

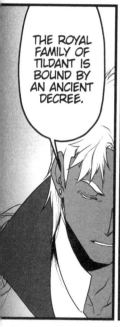

THE ROYAL FAMILY OF TILDANT IS BOUND BY AN ANCIENT DECREE.

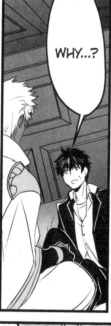

WHY...?

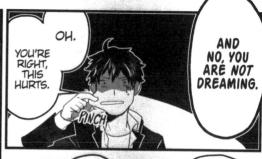

OH. YOU'RE RIGHT, THIS HURTS.

PINCH

AND NO, YOU ARE *NOT* DREAMING.

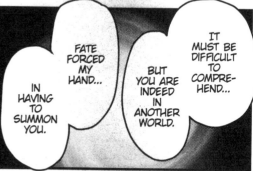

IN HAVING TO SUMMON YOU.

FATE FORCED MY HAND...

BUT YOU ARE INDEED IN ANOTHER WORLD.

IT MUST BE DIFFICULT TO COMPREHEND...

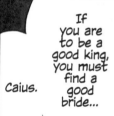

Caius.

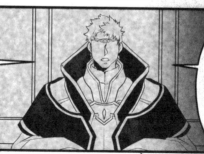

If you are to be a good king, you must find a good bride...

As such, his bride must come from a kingdom other than his own.

The king is the hallmark of prosperity.

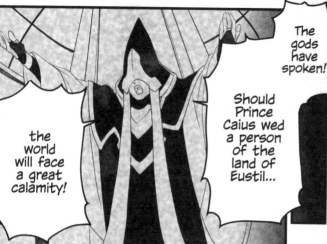

The gods have spoken!

Should Prince Caius wed a person of the land of Eustil...

the world will face a great calamity!

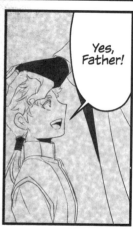

Yes, Father!

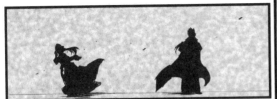

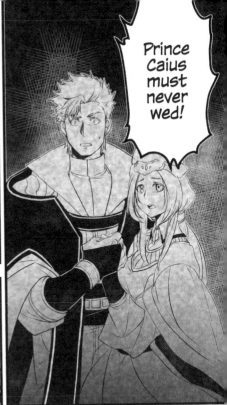

Prince Caius must never wed!

Up in the mage's tower once again, I fear.

Where is Caius?

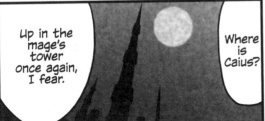

but that ritual was lost long ago.

No soul alive knows it.

We once could summon denizens of other worlds...

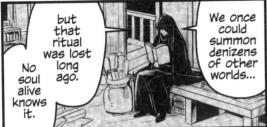

I will not give up on my search.

If it were possible once...

then it can be done again.

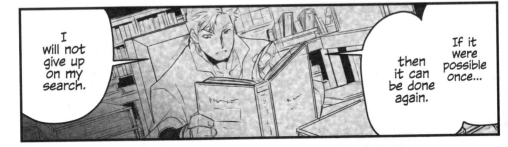

I SHALL HAVE BOTH!

AND I WILL BE WED.

I WILL BE KING...

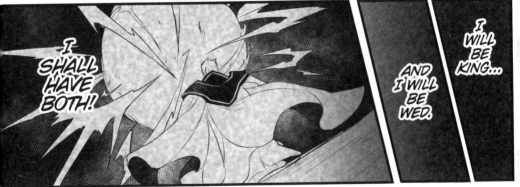

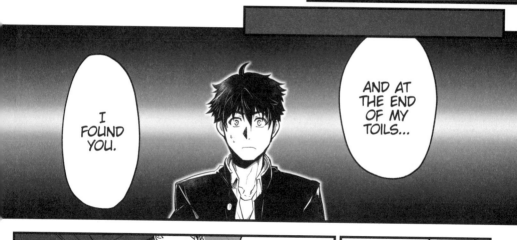

AND AT THE END OF MY TOILS...

I FOUND YOU.

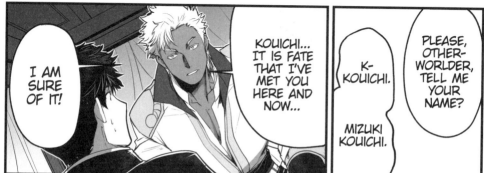

I AM SURE OF IT!

KOUICHI... IT IS FATE THAT I'VE MET YOU HERE AND NOW...

K-KOUICHI.

MIZUKI KOUICHI.

PLEASE, OTHER-WORLDER, TELL ME YOUR NAME?

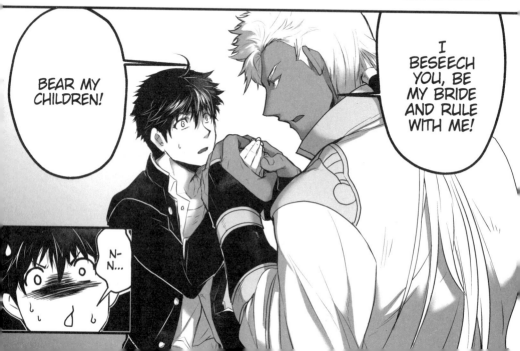

BEAR MY CHILDREN!

I BESEECH YOU, BE MY BRIDE AND RULE WITH ME!

N-N...

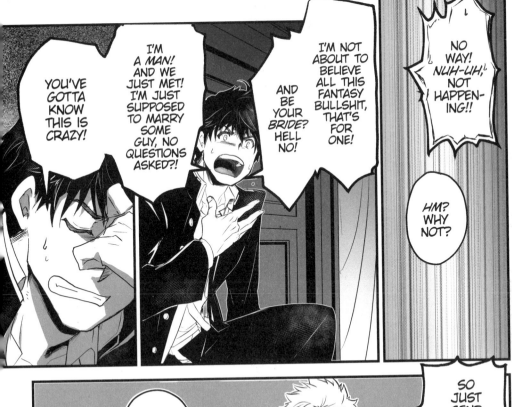

YOU'VE GOTTA KNOW THIS IS CRAZY!

I'M A *MAN!* AND WE JUST MET! I'M JUST SUPPOSED TO MARRY SOME GUY, NO QUESTIONS ASKED?!

AND BE YOUR *BRIDE?* HELL NO!

I'M NOT ABOUT TO BELIEVE ALL THIS FANTASY BULLSHIT, THAT'S FOR ONE!

NO WAY! *NUH-UH,* NOT HAPPEN-ING!!

HM? WHY NOT?

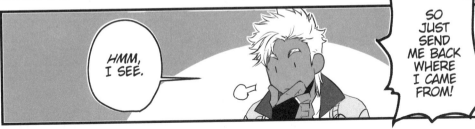

HMM, I SEE.

SO JUST SEND ME BACK WHERE I CAME FROM!

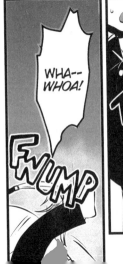

WHA-- WHOA!

FWUMP

TAP

EEP! JOLT

HE'S HUGE!

LOOM

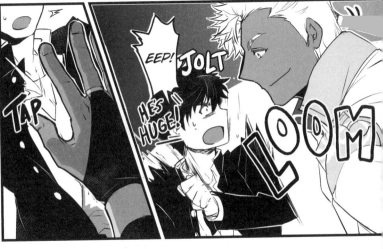

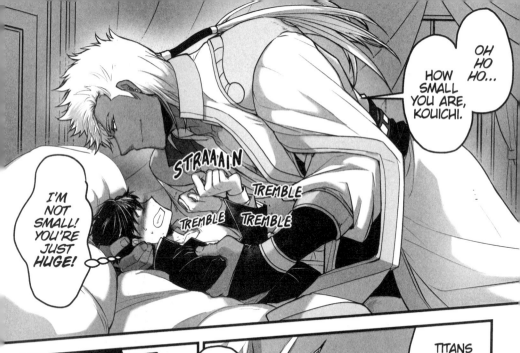

OH HO HO... HOW SMALL YOU ARE, KOUICHI.

I'M NOT SMALL! YOU'RE JUST HUGE!

STRAAAIN

TREMBLE

TREMBLE TREMBLE

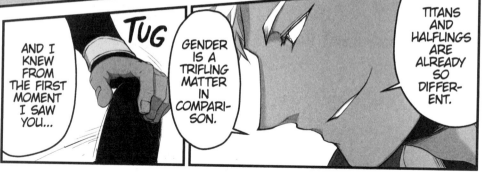

AND I KNEW FROM THE FIRST MOMENT I SAW YOU...

TUG

GENDER IS A TRIFLING MATTER IN COMPARISON.

TITANS AND HALFLINGS ARE ALREADY SO DIFFERENT.

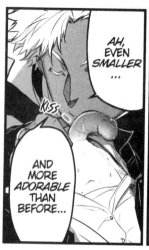

AH, EVEN SMALLER...

KISS

AND MORE ADORABLE THAN BEFORE...

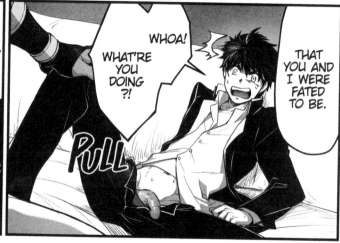

WHOA!

WHAT'RE YOU DOING ?!

PULL

THAT YOU AND I WERE FATED TO BE.

YOU WERE IN THE MIDST OF PLEASURING YOURSELF, YES?
ALLOW ME TO ASSIST.
AH!
UWAH!
SQUELCH
SQUELCH
SQUELCH
SQUELCH
TWITCH
SQUELCH
SQUELCH
TWITCH
SQUELCH
QUIVER
NO...
ST- STOP!
AH!
NO!
LET ME GO!
AH... AH!
SQUELCH
SQUELCH
SQUELCH
KOUICHI.
...?!
SHF
MN!
KISS
MM...
AH!
SLRP
SLP
LICK
HAAAH ...

HIS TONGUE IS HUGE, TOO...!
MNH!
NN!
KISS
KISS
HNG!
SHF
SQUELCH
SQUELCH
SQUELCH
SQUELCH
SQUELCH
GRIP
IS THIS WHAT IT FEELS LIKE...TO MAKE OUT WITH A GIANT?
TWITCH
TWITCH
LICK
HYAH?!
JOLT
AH!
HAH!
HAH!
SLP
SLURP
SLURP
DON'T SUCK ON MY...!
SQUELCH
SQUELCH
SQUELCH
I'M USING ALL MY STRENGTH AGAINST HIM...
NO!
AH!
BUT HE WON'T EVEN BUDGE!
DON'T!
SQUELCH
SQUELCH
SQUELCH
TREMBLE
AH!
AH!
TWITCH
TWITCH

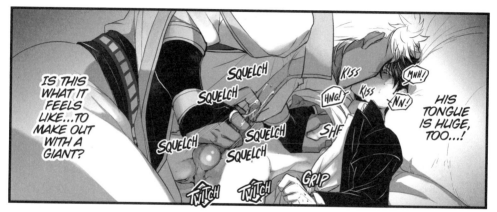

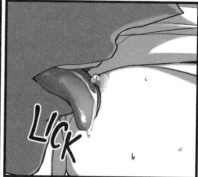

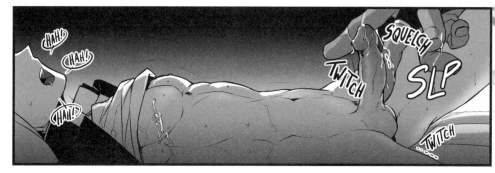

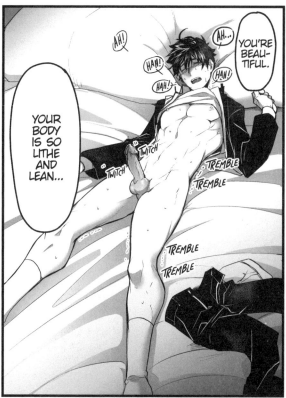

YOUR BODY IS SO LITHE AND LEAN...

YOU'RE BEAUTIFUL.

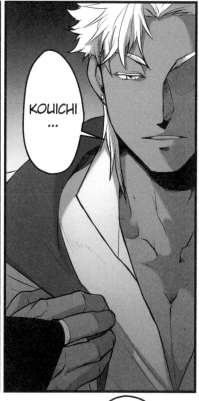

KOUICHI...

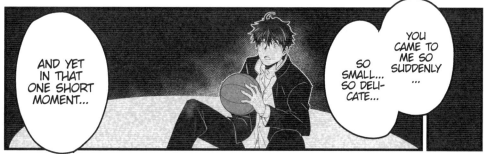

AND YET IN THAT ONE SHORT MOMENT...

SO SMALL... SO DELICATE...

YOU CAME TO ME SO SUDDENLY...

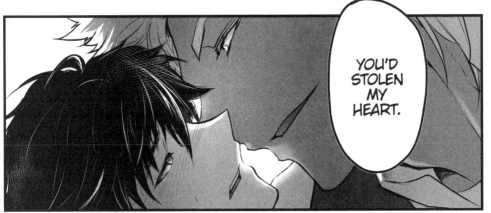

YOU'D STOLEN MY HEART.

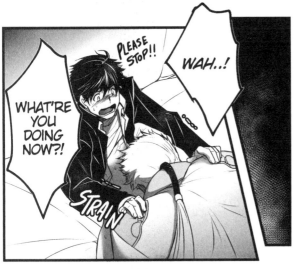

PLEASE STOP!!

WAH..!

WHAT'RE YOU DOING NOW?!

STRAIN

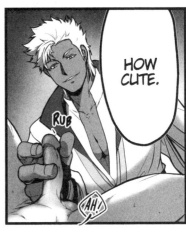

HOW CUTE.

RUB

AH!

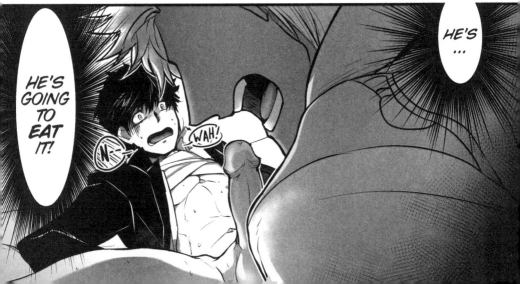

HE'S GOING TO EAT IT!

WAH!

HE'S ...

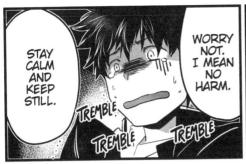

STAY CALM AND KEEP STILL.

WORRY NOT. I MEAN NO HARM.

TREMBLE
TREMBLE
TREMBLE

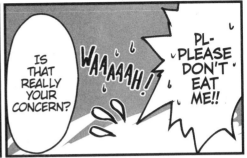

IS THAT REALLY YOUR CONCERN?

WAAAAAH!

PL- PLEASE DON'T EAT ME!!

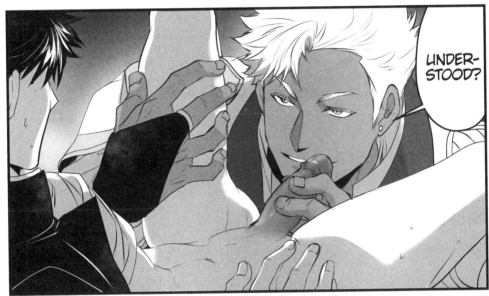

UNDER- STOOD?

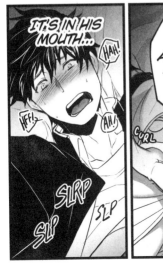

IT'S IN HIS MOUTH...

HAH!

HFF!

AH!

SLRP
SLP
SLP

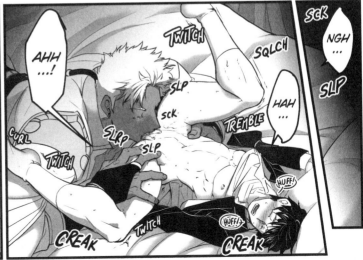

AHH ....!

TWITCH

SQLCH

SLP

sck

HAH ...

CURL

SLRP

TWITCH

SLP

TREMBLE

HUFF!

CREAK

TWITCH

CREAK

HUFF!

SCK

NGH ...

SLP

HIS LIPS AND TONGUE ARE HUGE...
SCK
SLP
SLRP
AND HE'S WRAPPING HIS TONGUE AROUND ME...
AH!
SCK
SLRP
AND DESPITE EVERYTHING, IT...
AH!
TWITCH
BWAH!
A...
AH!
HUFF!
HAAH!
IT FEELS GOOD...
HAH!
SLP
GH!
TWITCH
SLRP
SLP
CREAK
CLENCH
AH!
CREAK
TWITCH
CREAK
CURL
AH!
CLENCH
DON'T SUCK SO HARD, OR I'LL--
SLUUUURP
I'M--!
THROB
THROB

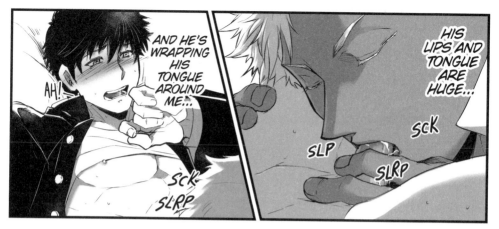

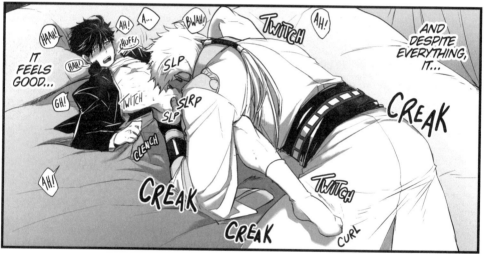

AGH!
THROB
SPURT
SPURT
I'M CUMMING!
HAAH...
HAAH...
YOU SEEM SO FRAGILE ...
AS IF A SIMPLE TOUCH WOULD BREAK YOU...
CLINK
SHFFL
HAH!
HAH!
SHUFF
HAH!
HAAH...
CREAK
KOUICHI...

I WANT YOU TO TAKE ALL OF ME.
AH...
NO...
TWITCH

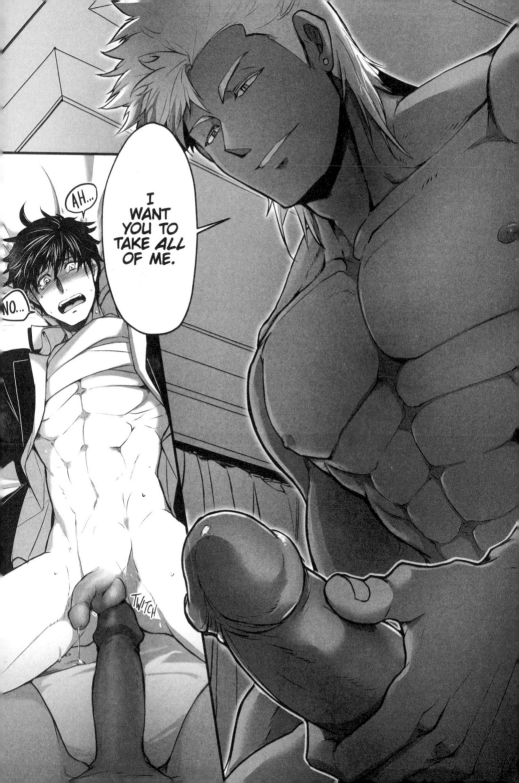

Chapter 2

CREAK
SHNF.
HIC!
PLEASE, DON'T...
IT WON'T FIT...
SOB!
DRIP
I'M SCARED...
HIC!
DRIP
FIRST, I GET DRAGGED TO A TOTALLY DIFFERENT WORLD...
SOB
SOB
NOW I'M GONNA GET FUCKED BY A GIANT AND DIE? I DON'T WANT TO DIE!

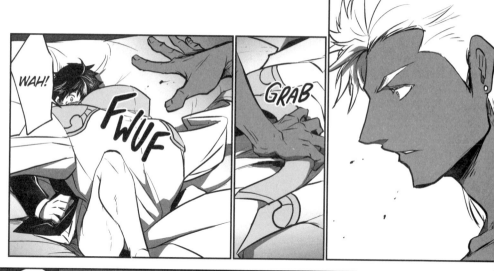

WAH!

FWUF

GRAB

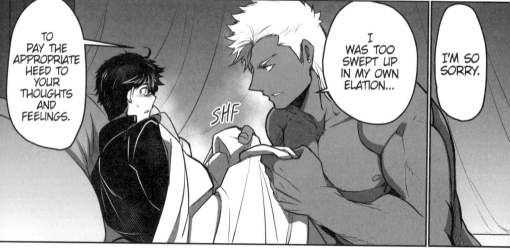

TO PAY THE APPROPRIATE HEED TO YOUR THOUGHTS AND FEELINGS.

SHF

I WAS TOO SWEPT UP IN MY OWN ELATION...

I'M SO SORRY.

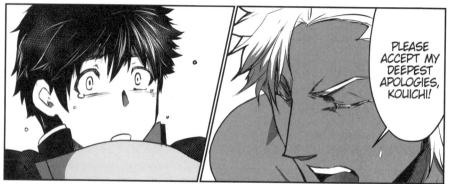

PLEASE ACCEPT MY DEEPEST APOLOGIES, KOUICHI!

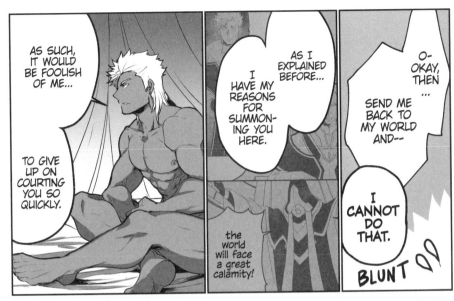

AS SUCH, IT WOULD BE FOOLISH OF ME...

TO GIVE UP ON COURTING YOU SO QUICKLY.

AS I EXPLAINED BEFORE...

I HAVE MY REASONS FOR SUMMON-ING YOU HERE.

the world will face a great calamity!

O-OKAY, THEN ...

SEND ME BACK TO MY WORLD AND--

I CANNOT DO THAT.

BLUNT

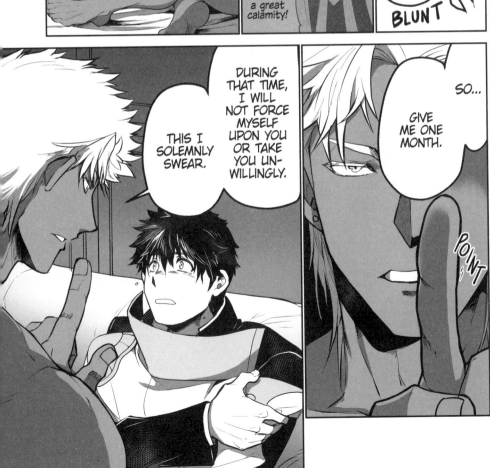

DURING THAT TIME, I WILL NOT FORCE MYSELF UPON YOU OR TAKE YOU UN-WILLINGLY.

THIS I SOLEMNLY SWEAR.

SO...

GIVE ME ONE MONTH.

POINT

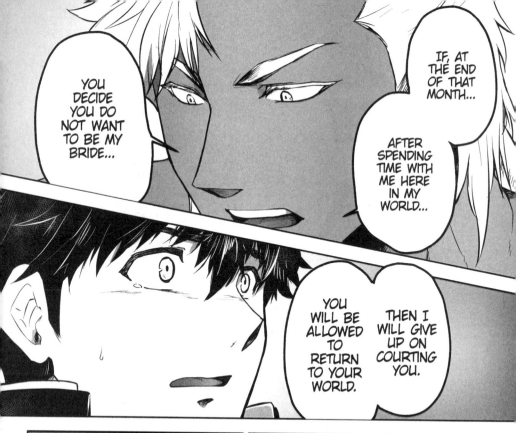

YOU DECIDE YOU DO NOT WANT TO BE MY BRIDE...

IF, AT THE END OF THAT MONTH...

AFTER SPENDING TIME WITH ME HERE IN MY WORLD...

YOU WILL BE ALLOWED TO RETURN TO YOUR WORLD.

THEN I WILL GIVE UP ON COURTING YOU.

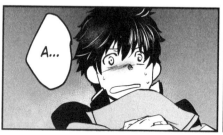

A...

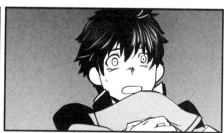

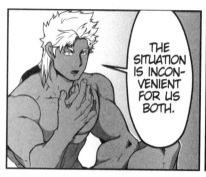

THE SITUATION IS INCONVENIENT FOR US BOTH.

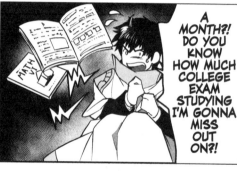

A MONTH?! DO YOU KNOW HOW MUCH COLLEGE EXAM STUDYING I'M GONNA MISS OUT ON?!

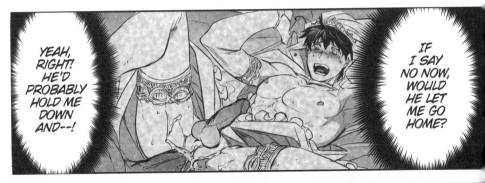

YEAH, RIGHT! HE'D PROBABLY HOLD ME DOWN AND--!

IF I SAY NO NOW, WOULD HE LET ME GO HOME?

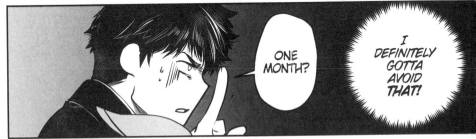

ONE MONTH?

I DEFINITELY GOTTA AVOID *THAT*!

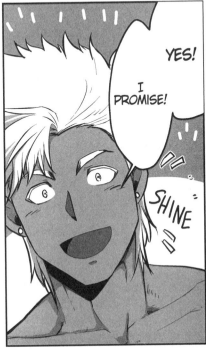

YES! I PROMISE!

SHINE

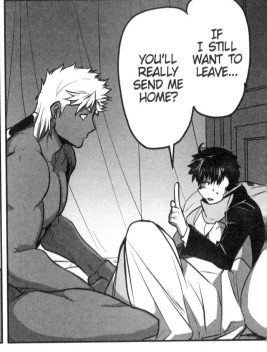

YOU'LL REALLY SEND ME HOME?

IF I STILL WANT TO LEAVE...

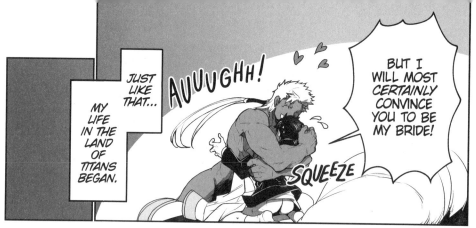

MY LIFE IN THE LAND OF TITANS BEGAN.

JUST LIKE THAT...

AUUUGHH!

BUT I WILL MOST CERTAINLY CONVINCE YOU TO BE MY BRIDE!

SQUEEZE

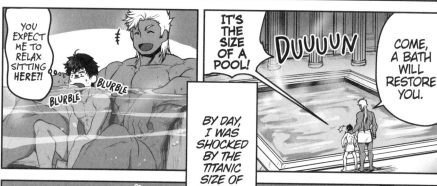

YOU EXPECT ME TO RELAX SITTING HERE?!

BLURBLE

BLURBLE

BLURBLE

IT'S THE SIZE OF A POOL!

DUUUUN

COME, A BATH WILL RESTORE YOU.

BY DAY, I WAS SHOCKED BY THE TITANIC SIZE OF IT ALL.

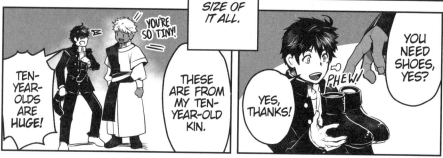

YOU'RE SO TINY!

TEN-YEAR-OLDS ARE HUGE!

THESE ARE FROM MY TEN-YEAR-OLD KIN.

PHEW!

YES, THANKS!

YOU NEED SHOES, YES?

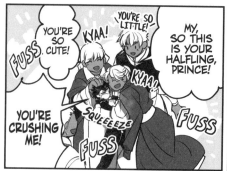

YOU'RE SO CUTE!

KYAA!

YOU'RE SO LITTLE!

MY, SO THIS IS YOUR HALFLING, PRINCE!

FUSS

KYAA!

FUSS

YOU'RE CRUSHING ME!

SQUEEZE

FUSS

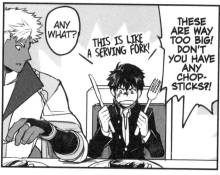

ANY WHAT?

THIS IS LIKE A SERVING FORK!

THESE ARE WAY TOO BIG! DON'T YOU HAVE ANY CHOP-STICKS?!

AND BY NIGHT...
HOLD A DAMN MINUTE!
YOU SAID YOU WEREN'T GONNA FORCE ME!
SMACK
HMM?
STRIP
STRIP
RELAX. I'M ONLY GOING TO GIVE YOU A MASSAGE.
YOU MUST BE EXHAUSTED FROM EVERYTHING THAT'S HAPPENED.
SLOSH
YEEEEK!!
COLD!
DRIBBLE
DRIP
JOLT
RELAX YOUR MUSCLES...
RUB
RUB
JUST LIKE THAT.

FEELS GOOD, YES?
SLP
RUB
RUB
SLP
YEAH, IT'S REALLY NICE.
THEN I'LL CONTINUE.
RUB
SLP
SLP
IT FEELS GOOD, BUT...
IT'S SO SLIPPERY.
HUFF...
SLP
RUB
SLP
RUB
OH, SHIT...
IT FEELS TOO GOOD.
MM...
TWITCH
SHIT...
SLP
SHUDDER
TWITCH
HAH...
HF...
I'M HARD.
HAH...
TWITCH
TWITCH

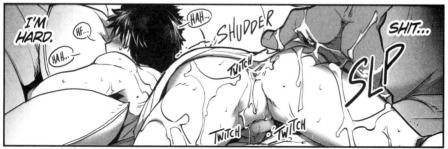

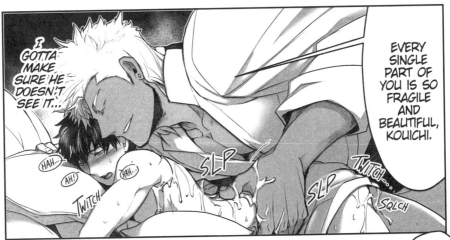

I GOTTA MAKE SURE HE DOESN'T SEE IT...

HAH...

AH!

HAH...

TWITCH

SLP

SLP

TWITCH...

SQLCH

EVERY SINGLE PART OF YOU IS SO FRAGILE AND BEAUTIFUL, KOUICHI.

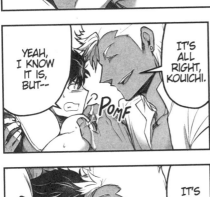

YEAH, I KNOW IT IS, BUT--

IT'S ALL RIGHT, KOUICHI.

POMF

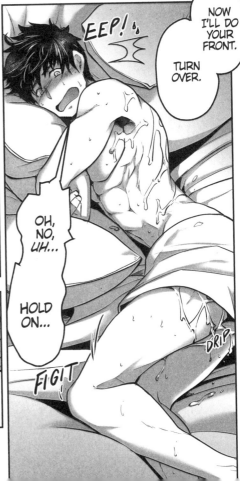

EEP!

NOW I'LL DO YOUR FRONT.

TURN OVER.

OH, NO, UH...

HOLD ON...

FIGIT

DRIP

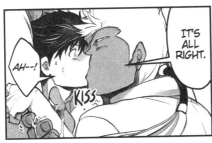

AH--!

IT'S ALL RIGHT.

KISS

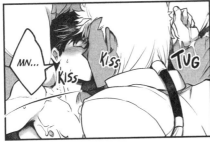

MN...

KISS

KISS

TUG

035

I SAID... N-NO...
DRIP
HAA!
HAH!
RUB
RUB
WAH!
TWITCH
SLP
SLP
RELAX. I WILL KEEP MY PROMISE.
BLUB
DRIBBLE
JUST CLOSE YOUR EYES...
HUFF.
TMP
HUFF.
AH!
KISS
LICK
KISS
FUH...
MM!
KISS
LICK
KISS
RUB
SLP
AND GIVE YOURSELF OVER TO PLEASURE.
SQLCH
SQLCH
SQLCH
TWITCH

SLP
SLP
POKE
POKE
PANIC
AH... HOLD ON, NOT THERE!
DON'T TOU--
SQLCH
SLIP!
HYAH... AHH!
AH... NO!
SHUDDER
SHUDDER
NO...!
NO!
AH!
AH!
AH!
YOU'RE GONNA RIP ME OPEN...!
TWITCH
TWITCH
SQUEEZE
SQLCH
SQLCH
THRUST
TWITCH
TWITCH
SQLCH
THRUST
TWITCH
THRUST
THRUST
SQLCH
SQLCH
SQLCH
AH!
IT'S ALL RIGHT.
IT'S JUST ONE FINGER.
HAH!
NO!

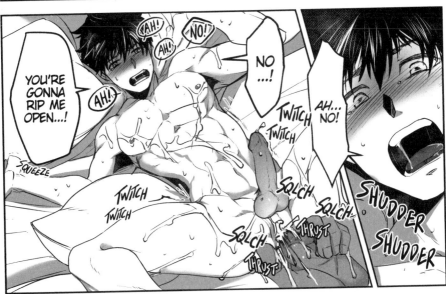

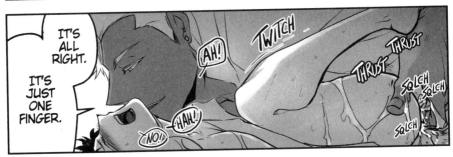

YOU'LL ADJUST TO IT QUICKLY.
SQLCH
TWITCH
RUB
RUB
SQLCH
AH!
HAH!
MNGH!
IT FEELS LIKE...
HAH!
JUST ONE FINGER?
IT'S HUGE...
TWITCH
IT'S PUSHING UP AGAINST ALL MY INSIDES...
GRIP
SQLCH
POKE
THRUST
SQLCH
TWITCH
THRUST
SQLCH
SQLCH
AH! NOT... NOT THERE!
NNGH!
SQLCH
SQLCH
SQLCH
THERE IS GOOD.
AH!
NO...!
AH!
NO!
IT'S...
TWITCH
WHAT IS THIS FEELING?!
I'M...
AH!
SOME-THING'S BUILDING UP INSIDE...
SHUDDER
TWITCH
TWITCH
TWITCH
SQLCH
SQLCH
SQLCH
SHUDDER
SHUDDER
SHUDDER
SHUDDER

AHHHHHH!
SPURT
SPRT
THROB
THROB
SHUDDER
SHUDDER
SHUDDER
SHUDDER
GRIP
SPLATTER
PAT
KOUICHI.
HUFF...
HUFF...
GRIN
TOMORROW, WE'LL TRY TWO FINGERS!

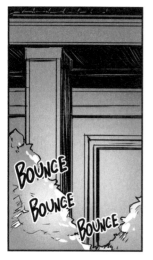

BOUNCE
BOUNCE
BOUNCE

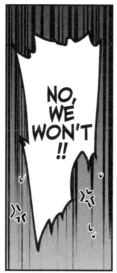

NO, WE WON'T!!

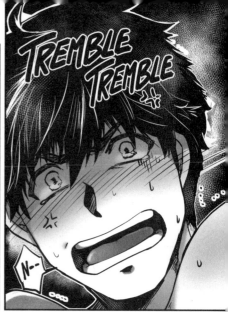

TREMBLE TREMBLE

N--

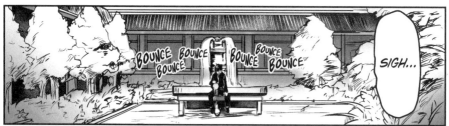

BOUNCE BOUNCE
BOUNCE
BOUNCE BOUNCE
BOUNCE

SIGH...

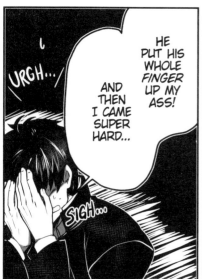

URGH...

HE PUT HIS WHOLE FINGER UP MY ASS!

AND THEN I CAME SUPER HARD...

SIGH...

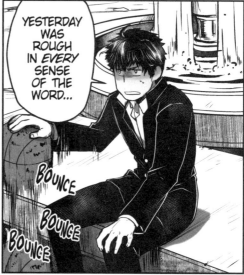

YESTERDAY WAS ROUGH IN EVERY SENSE OF THE WORD...

BOUNCE
BOUNCE
BOUNCE

AHHHHH!
SPURT
THROB
SHUDDER
TWITCH
I SHOULDN'T ...
UGH.
BLUSSSHH
AAAARGH!
NO, NUH-UH!
RRRRRGH!
WHAT THE HELL IS WRONG WITH ME?!
GETTING TURNED ON BY A GUY, AND CUMMING, TOO?!
BOUNCE
BOUNCE
BOUNCE
BOUNCE
BOUNCE
I AM NOT GAY! I LIKE WOMEN! I'M ONLY GETTING HORNY BECAUSE I'M A VIRGIN AND HAVEN'T GOT ANY SEXUAL EXPERIENCE! IT'S ONLY NORMAL THAT I'D GET TURNED ON! THE ONLY REASON I CAME FROM GETTING MY ASS PLAYED WITH WAS 'CAUSE IT FELT GOOD, AND I'M YOUNG AND
GASP
KOUICHI!
WHAT ARE YOU DOING OUT HERE?
CAIUS!

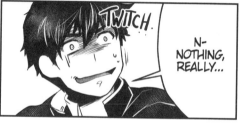

WHAT IS THAT BALL YOU CARRY WITH YOU?

N-NOTHING, REALLY...

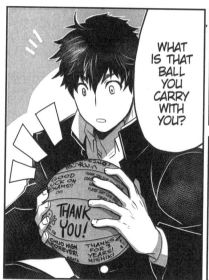

I'VE BEEN MEANING TO ASK YOU...

PLOP

I SEE.

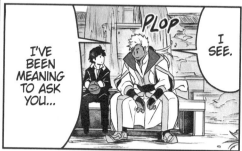

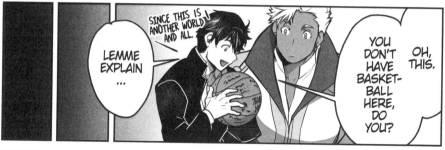

SINCE THIS IS ANOTHER WORLD AND ALL...

LEMME EXPLAIN...

YOU DON'T HAVE BASKET-BALL HERE, DO YOU?

OH, THIS.

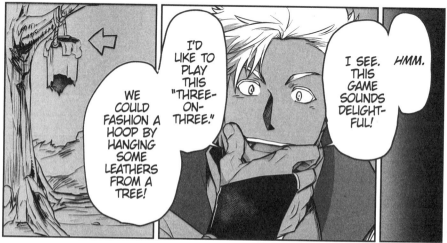

WE COULD FASHION A HOOP BY HANGING SOME LEATHERS FROM A TREE!

I'D LIKE TO PLAY THIS "THREE-ON-THREE."

I SEE. THIS GAME SOUNDS DELIGHT-FUL!

HMM.

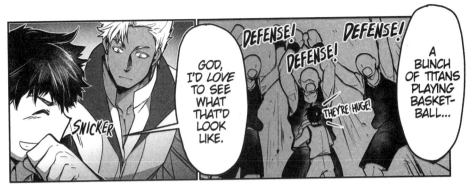

GOD, I'D LOVE TO SEE WHAT THAT'D LOOK LIKE.

SNICKER

DEFENSE! DEFENSE! DEFENSE!

THEY'RE HUGE!

A BUNCH OF TITANS PLAYING BASKET-BALL...

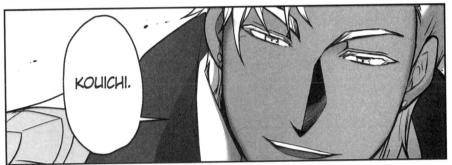

KOUICHI.

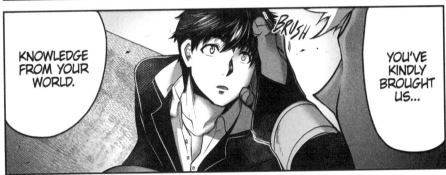

KNOWLEDGE FROM YOUR WORLD.

BRUSH

YOU'VE KINDLY BROUGHT US...

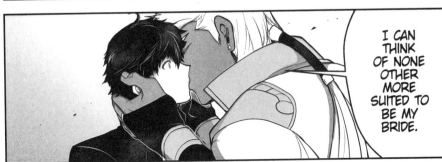

I CAN THINK OF NONE OTHER MORE SUITED TO BE MY BRIDE.

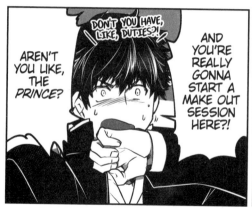

AREN'T YOU LIKE, THE *PRINCE*?

DON'T YOU HAVE, LIKE, DUTIES?!

AND YOU'RE REALLY GONNA START A MAKE OUT SESSION HERE?!

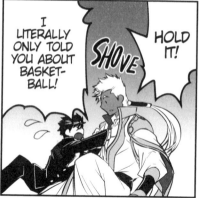

I LITERALLY ONLY TOLD YOU ABOUT BASKET-BALL!

HOLD IT!

SHOVE

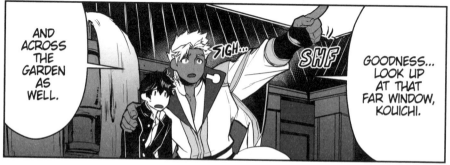

AND ACROSS THE GARDEN AS WELL.

SIGH...

SHF

GOODNESS... LOOK UP AT THAT FAR WINDOW, KOUICHI.

IT IS, INDEED, OUR DUTY!

IN OUR KINGDOM, WE WHOLE-HEARTEDLY ENCOURAGE ALL TO ENGAGE IN SEXUAL RELATIONS WHENEVER THEY SO PLEASE!

YOUR KINGDOM IS TAKING THAT WAY TOO FAR!

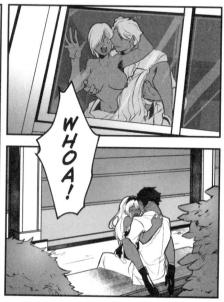

WHOA!

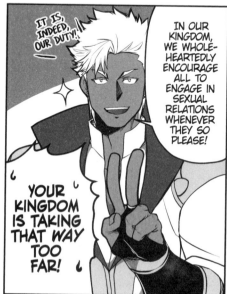

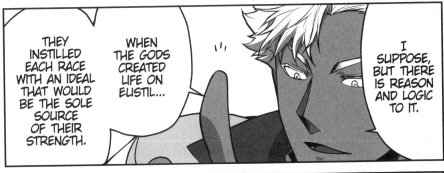

WHEN THE GODS CREATED LIFE ON ELISTIL...

THEY INSTILLED EACH RACE WITH AN IDEAL THAT WOULD BE THE SOLE SOURCE OF THEIR STRENGTH.

I SUPPOSE, BUT THERE IS REASON AND LOGIC TO IT.

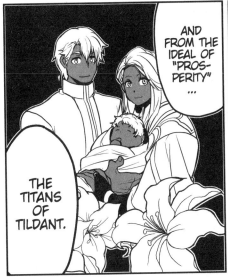

AND FROM THE IDEAL OF "PROS-PERITY"...

THE TITANS OF TILDANT.

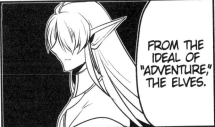

FROM THE IDEAL OF "ADVENTURE," THE ELVES.

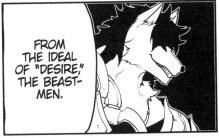

FROM THE IDEAL OF "DESIRE," THE BEAST-MEN.

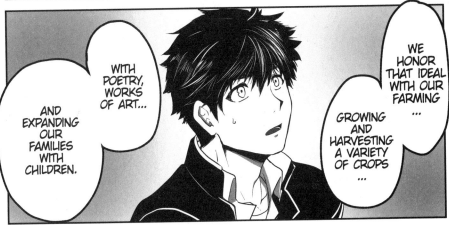

WITH POETRY, WORKS OF ART...

AND EXPANDING OUR FAMILIES WITH CHILDREN.

WE HONOR THAT IDEAL WITH OUR FARMING...

GROWING AND HARVESTING A VARIETY OF CROPS...

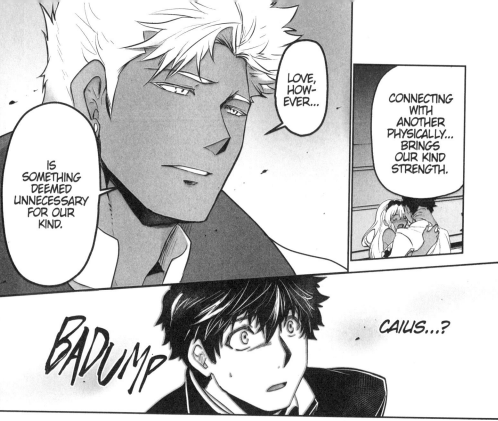

LOVE, HOW-EVER...

CONNECTING WITH ANOTHER PHYSICALLY... BRINGS OUR KIND STRENGTH.

IS SOMETHING DEEMED UNNECESSARY FOR OUR KIND.

BADUMP

CAIUS...?

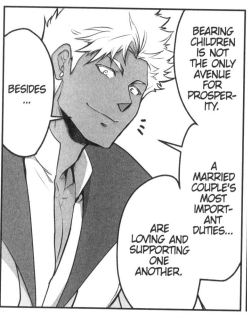

BESIDES...

BEARING CHILDREN IS NOT THE ONLY AVENUE FOR PROSPERITY.

A MARRIED COUPLE'S MOST IMPORTANT DUTIES...

ARE LOVING AND SUPPORTING ONE ANOTHER.

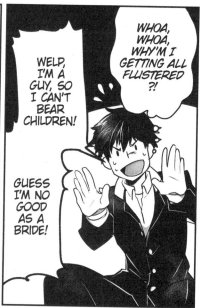

WHOA, WHOA, WHY'M I GETTING ALL FLUSTERED ?!

WELP, I'M A GUY, SO I CAN'T BEAR CHILDREN!

GUESS I'M NO GOOD AS A BRIDE!

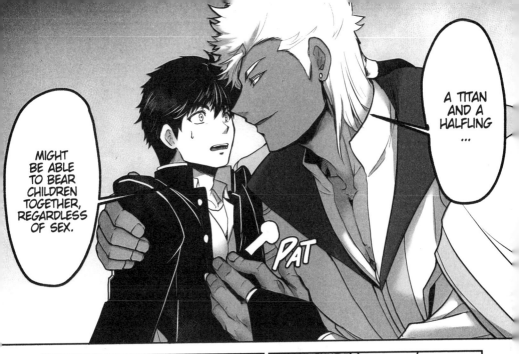

A TITAN AND A HALFLING...

MIGHT BE ABLE TO BEAR CHILDREN TOGETHER, REGARDLESS OF SEX.

PAT

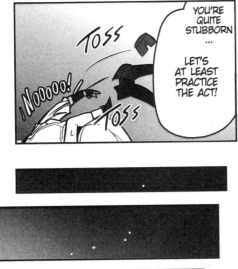

TOSS

NOOOOO!

TOSS

YOU'RE QUITE STUBBORN...

LET'S AT LEAST PRACTICE THE ACT!

AH!!

HAH!!

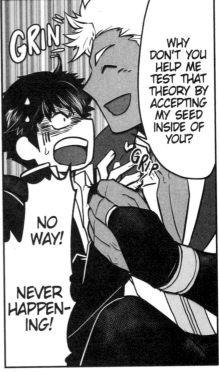

GRIN

WHY DON'T YOU HELP ME TEST THAT THEORY BY ACCEPTING MY SEED INSIDE OF YOU?

GRIP

NO WAY!

NEVER HAPPEN-ING!

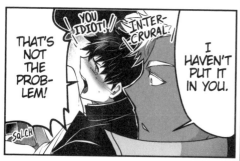

YOU IDIOT!

IN·TER·CRURAL.

THAT'S NOT THE PROBLEM!

I HAVEN'T PUT IT IN YOU.

SQLCH

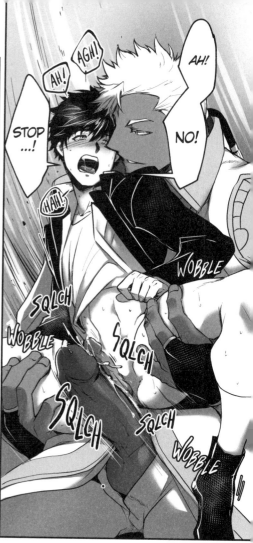

AH!

AGH!

AH!

STOP...!

NO!

HAH!

WOBBLE

SQLCH

WOBBLE

SQLCH

SQLCH

SQLCH

WOBBLE

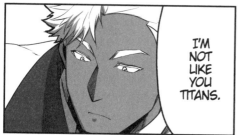

I'M NOT LIKE YOU TITANS.

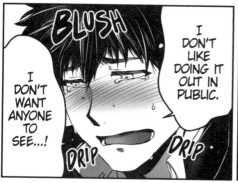

BLUSH

I DON'T WANT ANYONE TO SEE...!

I DON'T LIKE DOING IT OUT IN PUBLIC.

DRIP

DRIP

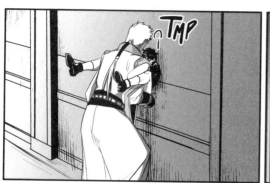

TMP

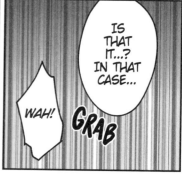

IS THAT IT...? IN THAT CASE...

WAH!

GRAB

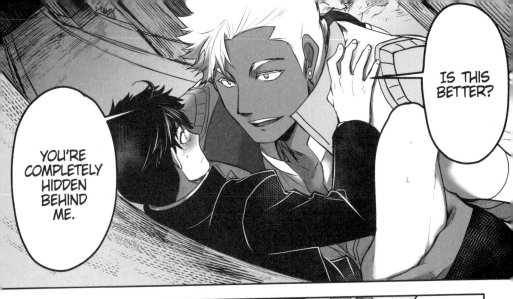

IS THIS BETTER?

YOU'RE COMPLETELY HIDDEN BEHIND ME.

WIPE

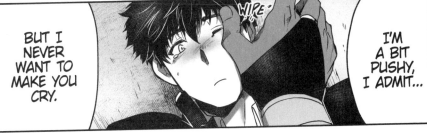

BUT I NEVER WANT TO MAKE YOU CRY.

I'M A BIT PUSHY, I ADMIT...

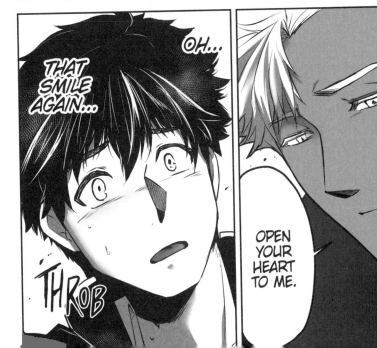

OH...

THAT SMILE AGAIN...

SO PLEASE, KOUICHI...

OPEN YOUR HEART TO ME.

THROB

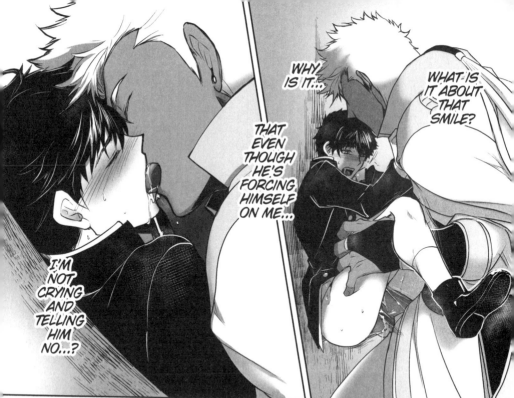

WHY IS IT...

WHAT IS IT ABOUT THAT SMILE?

THAT EVEN THOUGH HE'S FORCING HIMSELF ON ME...

I'M NOT CRYING AND TELLING HIM NO...?

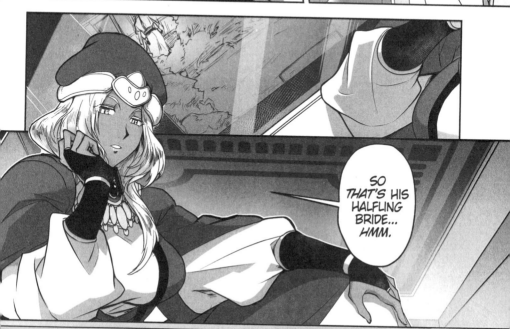

SO THAT'S HIS HALFLING BRIDE... HMM.

FIND YOUR SOULMATE!
ISEKAI SUMMON GACHA
1 Pull
530,000
GRAB YOURSELF A CUTE STUDENT!
NOW WITH A HIGHER CHANCE TO PULL
5-STAR MIZUKI KOUICHI!
DETAILS
PULL ODDS

BLING!
NEW
WAIT, WHA... WHAT THE HELL?
THE HELL IS THIS?!
BWOOOOOOSH
MIZUKI KOUICHI

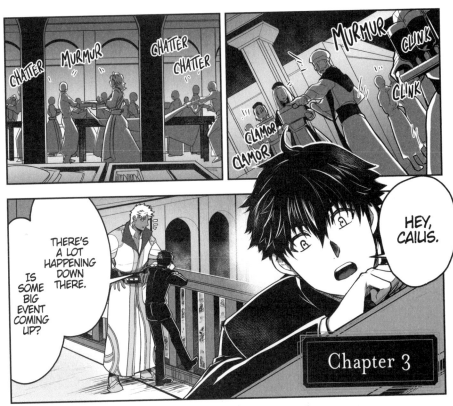

CHATTER MURMUR CHATTER CHATTER

MURMUR CLINK CLINK

CLAMOR CLAMOR

HEY, CAIUS.

THERE'S A LOT HAPPENING DOWN THERE.

IS SOME BIG EVENT COMING UP?

Chapter 3

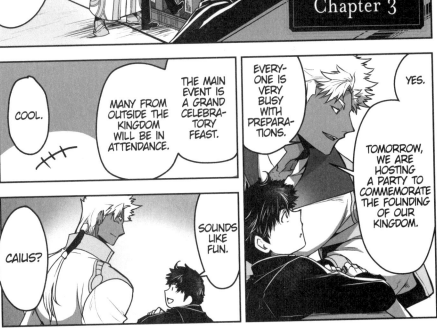

THE MAIN EVENT IS A GRAND CELEBRATORY FEAST.

MANY FROM OUTSIDE THE KINGDOM WILL BE IN ATTENDANCE.

COOL.

EVERYONE IS VERY BUSY WITH PREPARATIONS.

YES.

TOMORROW, WE ARE HOSTING A PARTY TO COMMEMORATE THE FOUNDING OF OUR KINGDOM.

CAIUS?

SOUNDS LIKE FUN.

IT'S BEEN TOO LONG.
FLUTTER
MEDINA!
?
HOW ARE YOU? I MUST SAY, YOU'RE AS BEAUTIFUL AS EVER!
HUG
MY, I WAS JUST ABOUT TO TELL YOU HOW MUCH MORE HANDSOME YOU'VE GROWN!
WHO'S SHE?
AWKWARD...
THEY SEEM PRETTY CLOSE...
OH, WHO IS THAT WITH YOU?
MY APOLOGIES, LET ME INTRODUCE YOU.
THIS IS KOUICHI.

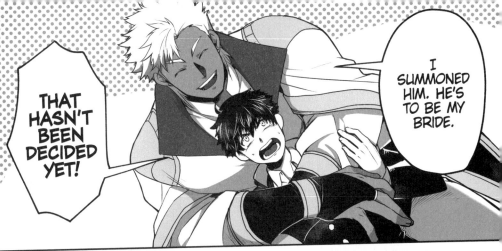

THAT HASN'T BEEN DECIDED YET!

I SUMMONED HIM. HE'S TO BE MY BRIDE.

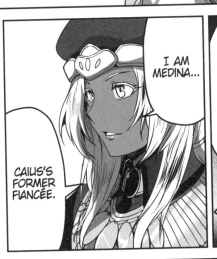

I AM MEDINA...

CAIUS'S FORMER FIANCÉE.

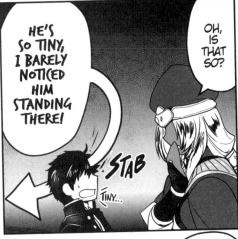

HE'S SO TINY, I BARELY NOTICED HIM STANDING THERE!

OH, IS THAT SO?

STAB

TINY...

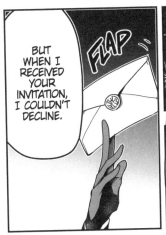

BUT WHEN I RECEIVED YOUR INVITATION, I COULDN'T DECLINE.

FLAP

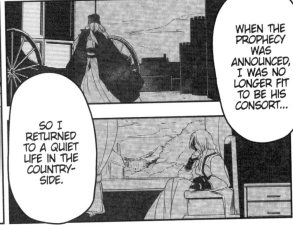

SO I RETURNED TO A QUIET LIFE IN THE COUNTRY-SIDE.

WHEN THE PROPHECY WAS ANNOUNCED, I WAS NO LONGER FIT TO BE HIS CONSORT...

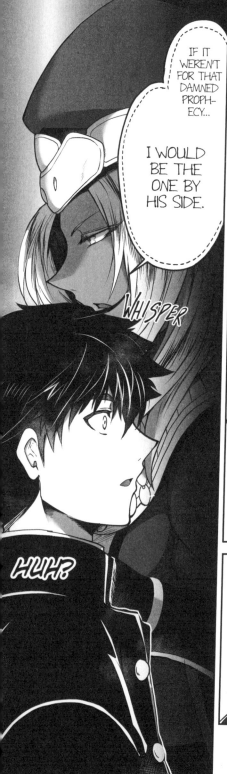

IF IT WEREN'T FOR THAT DAMNED PROPHECY...

I WOULD BE THE ONE BY HIS SIDE.

WHISPER

HUH?

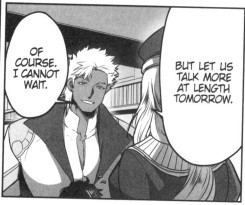

OF COURSE. I CANNOT WAIT.

BUT LET US TALK MORE AT LENGTH TOMORROW.

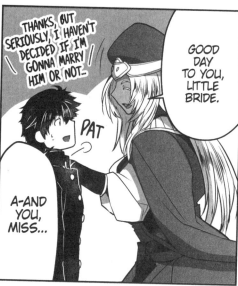

THANKS, BUT SERIOUSLY, I HAVEN'T DECIDED IF I'M GONNA MARRY HIM OR NOT...

GOOD DAY TO YOU, LITTLE BRIDE.

PAT

A-AND YOU, MISS...

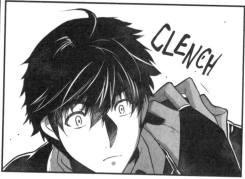

CLENCH

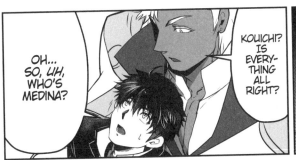

OH... SO, UH, WHO'S MEDINA?

KOUICHI? IS EVERY-THING ALL RIGHT?

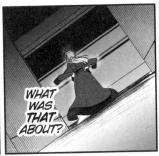

WHAT WAS THAT ABOUT?

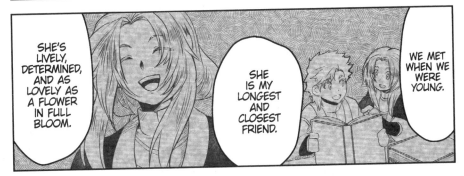

SHE'S LIVELY, DETERMINED, AND AS LOVELY AS A FLOWER IN FULL BLOOM.

SHE IS MY LONGEST AND CLOSEST FRIEND.

WE MET WHEN WE WERE YOUNG.

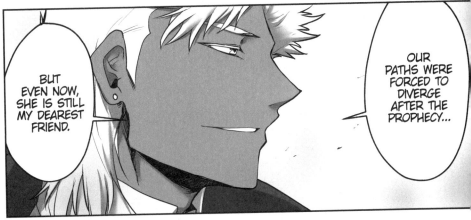

BUT EVEN NOW, SHE IS STILL MY DEAREST FRIEND.

OUR PATHS WERE FORCED TO DIVERGE AFTER THE PROPHECY...

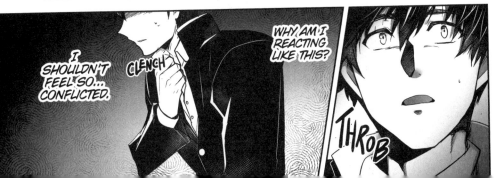

I SHOULDN'T FEEL SO... CONFLICTED.

CLENCH

WHY AM I REACTING LIKE THIS?

THROB

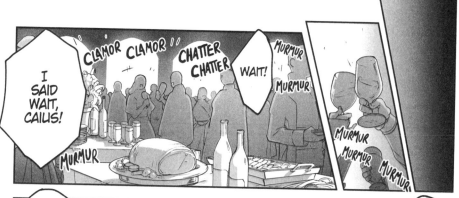

CLAMOR CLAMOR

CHATTER CHATTER

WAIT!

MURMUR

MURMUR

I SAID WAIT, CAIUS!

MURMUR

MURMUR MURMUR

MURMUR MURMUR

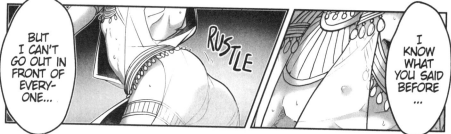

BUT I CAN'T GO OUT IN FRONT OF EVERY-ONE...

RUSTLE

I KNOW WHAT YOU SAID BEFORE ...

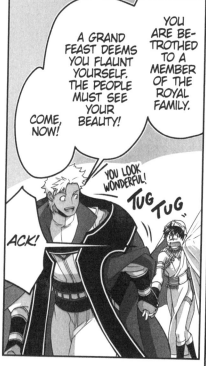

YOU ARE BE-TROTHED TO A MEMBER OF THE ROYAL FAMILY.

A GRAND FEAST DEEMS YOU FLAUNT YOURSELF. THE PEOPLE MUST SEE YOUR BEAUTY!

COME, NOW!

YOU LOOK WONDERFUL!

TUG TUG

ACK!

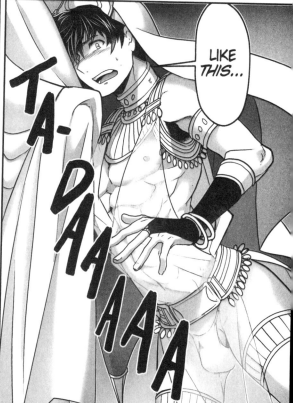

TA-DAAAAA

LIKE THIS...

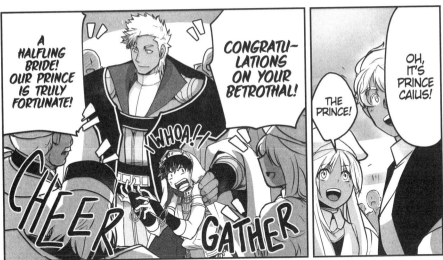

A HALFLING BRIDE! OUR PRINCE IS TRULY FORTUNATE!

CONGRATU- LATIONS ON YOUR BETROTHAL!

WHOA!!

CHEER

GATHER

THE PRINCE!

OH, IT'S PRINCE CAIUS!

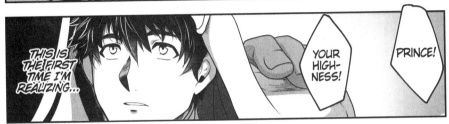

THIS IS THE FIRST TIME I'M REALIZING...

YOUR HIGH- NESS!

PRINCE!

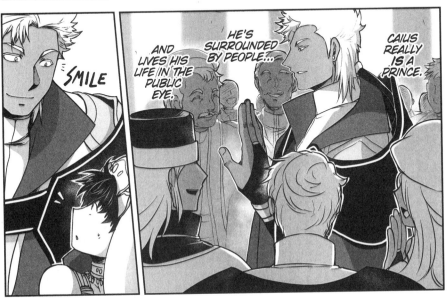

SMILE

AND LIVES HIS LIFE IN THE PUBLIC EYE.

HE'S SURROUNDED BY PEOPLE....

CAIUS REALLY IS A PRINCE.

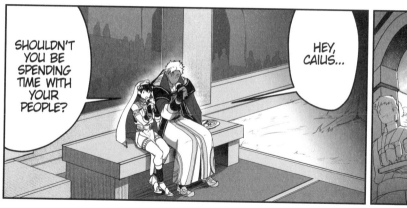

SHOULDN'T YOU BE SPENDING TIME WITH YOUR PEOPLE?

HEY, CAILUS...

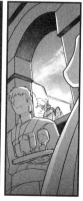

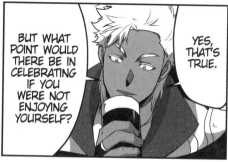

BUT WHAT POINT WOULD THERE BE IN CELEBRATING IF YOU WERE NOT ENJOYING YOURSELF?

YES, THAT'S TRUE.

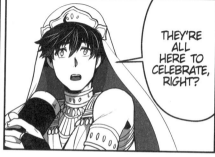

THEY'RE ALL HERE TO CELEBRATE, RIGHT?

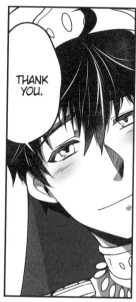

THANK YOU.

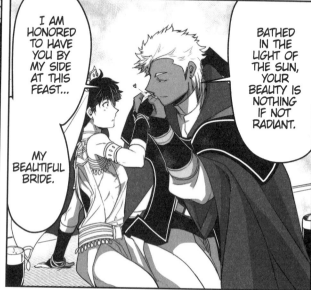

I AM HONORED TO HAVE YOU BY MY SIDE AT THIS FEAST...

MY BEAUTIFUL BRIDE.

BATHED IN THE LIGHT OF THE SUN, YOUR BEAUTY IS NOTHING IF NOT RADIANT.

IT'S MEDINA NALL ROSAS.

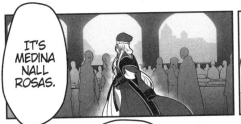

HEY, LOOK AT THAT.

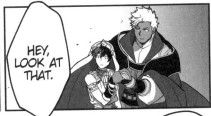

BUT THE MOMENT THAT PROPHECY WAS READ, THE TRAITOR ABANDONED HIM!

SHE WAS SO ATTACHED TO CAIUS...

HAS SHE NO SHAME?

MURMUR
MURMUR
MURMUR
MURMUR

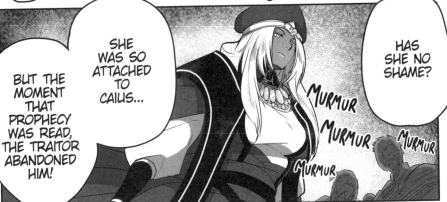

BOLD OF THE HARLOT TO SHOW HER FACE IN THE CAPITAL.

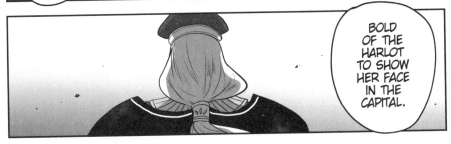

WAIT HERE, KOUICHI!

FWIP

IS THAT... MEDINA?

TEP

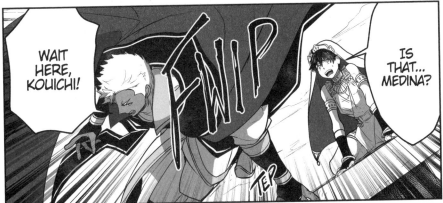

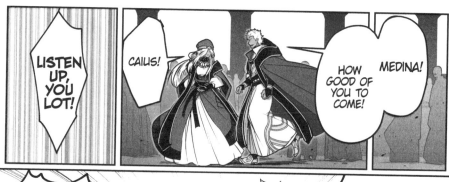

LISTEN UP, YOU LOT!

CAIUS!

HOW GOOD OF YOU TO COME!

MEDINA!

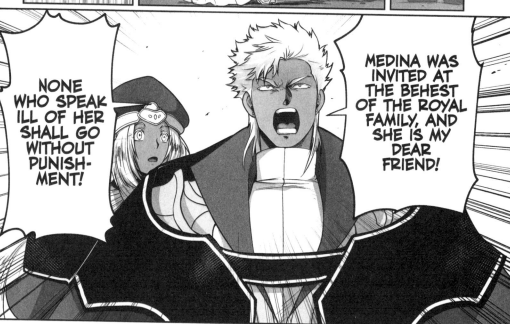

NONE WHO SPEAK ILL OF HER SHALL GO WITHOUT PUNISH-MENT!

MEDINA WAS INVITED AT THE BEHEST OF THE ROYAL FAMILY, AND SHE IS MY DEAR FRIEND!

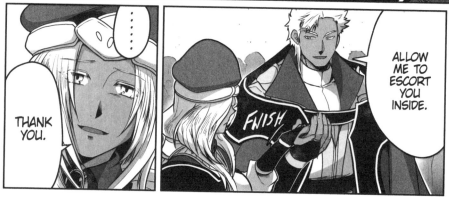

THANK YOU.

FINISH

ALLOW ME TO ESCORT YOU INSIDE.

"I WOULD BE THE ONE BY HIS SIDE."

"IF IT WEREN'T FOR THAT DAMNED PROPHECY..."

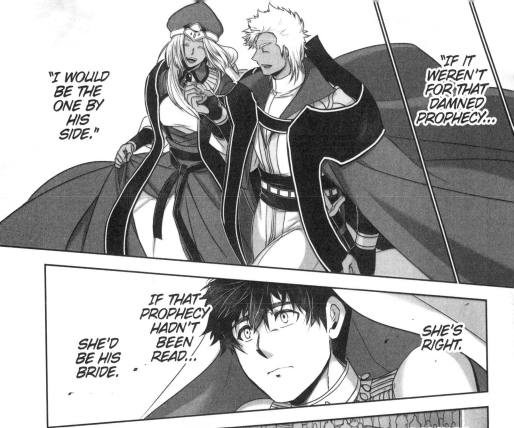

IF THAT PROPHECY HADN'T BEEN READ...

SHE'D BE HIS BRIDE.

SHE'S RIGHT.

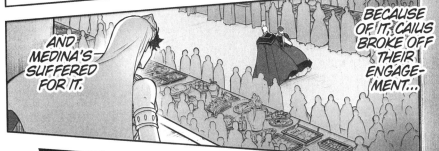

AND MEDINA'S SUFFERED FOR IT.

BECAUSE OF IT, CAIUS BROKE OFF THEIR ENGAGE-MENT...

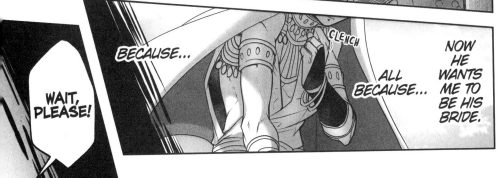

BECAUSE...

CLENCH

ALL BECAUSE...

NOW HE WANTS ME TO BE HIS BRIDE.

WAIT, PLEASE!

YOU'VE DECIDED YOU WILL NOT BE MY BRIDE?
THERE'S STILL PLENTY OF TIME BEFORE THE END OF OUR MONTH!
IF YOU'VE ANY QUALMS OR COMPLAINTS, I WOULD LIKE TO HEAR THEM--
I DON'T! THAT'S NOT WHY I'M SAYING THAT!
YOU'VE TREATED ME VERY WELL, CAIUS.
......
DID I HEAR YOU CORRECTLY, KOUICHI?
BUT I THINK...
YOU SHOULD MARRY THE PERSON YOU TRULY LOVE.

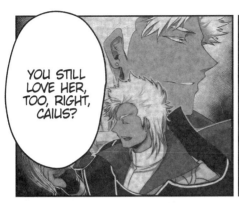

YOU STILL LOVE HER, TOO, RIGHT, CAIUS?

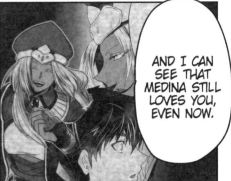

AND I CAN SEE THAT MEDINA STILL LOVES YOU, EVEN NOW.

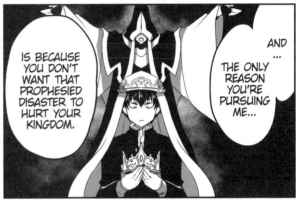

YOU SAID YOU SUMMONED ME BECAUSE YOU WANTED TO GET BOTH THE THRONE...

AND TRUE LOVE...

IS BECAUSE YOU DON'T WANT THAT PROPHESIED DISASTER TO HURT YOUR KINGDOM.

AND... THE ONLY REASON YOU'RE PURSUING ME...

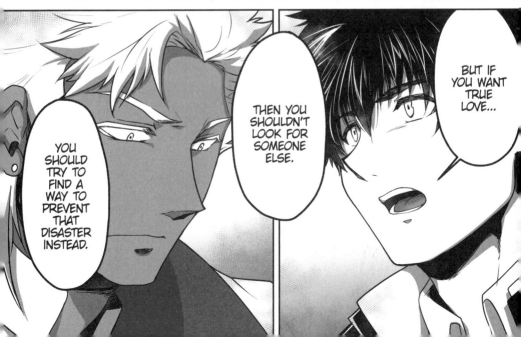

YOU SHOULD TRY TO FIND A WAY TO PREVENT THAT DISASTER INSTEAD.

THEN YOU SHOULDN'T LOOK FOR SOMEONE ELSE.

BUT IF YOU WANT TRUE LOVE...

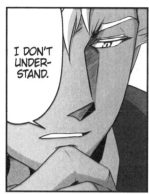

I DON'T UNDER-STAND.

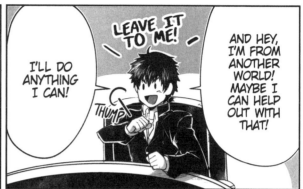

I'LL DO ANYTHING I CAN!

LEAVE IT TO ME!

THUMP

AND HEY, I'M FROM ANOTHER WORLD! MAYBE I CAN HELP OUT WITH THAT!

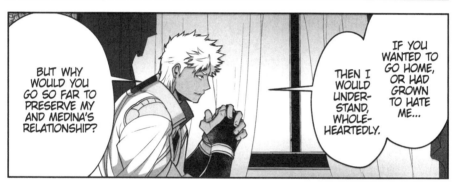

BUT WHY WOULD YOU GO SO FAR TO PRESERVE MY AND MEDINA'S RELATIONSHIP?

THEN I WOULD UNDER-STAND, WHOLE-HEARTEDLY.

IF YOU WANTED TO GO HOME, OR HAD GROWN TO HATE ME...

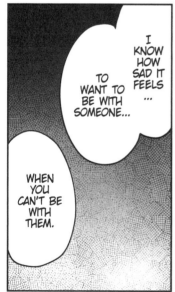

I KNOW HOW SAD IT FEELS ...

TO WANT TO BE WITH SOMEONE...

WHEN YOU CAN'T BE WITH THEM.

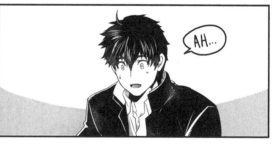

AH...

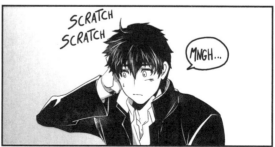

SCRATCH SCRATCH

MNGH...

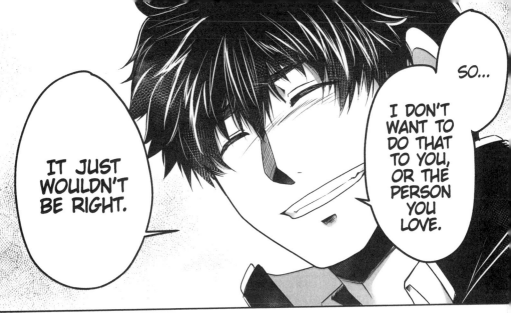

SO...

I DON'T WANT TO DO THAT TO YOU, OR THE PERSON YOU LOVE.

IT JUST WOULDN'T BE RIGHT.

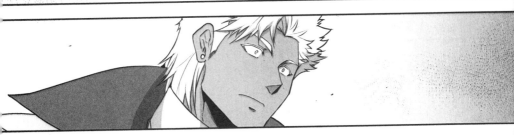

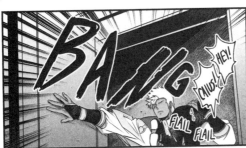

BANG

HEY!

CHUS!

FLAIL FLAIL

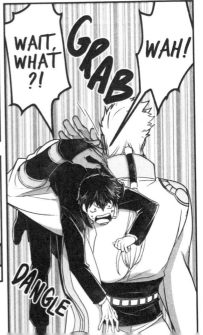

WAIT, WHAT ?!

GRAB

WAH!

DANGLE

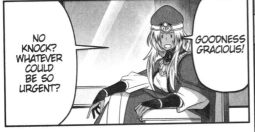

NO KNOCK? WHATEVER COULD BE SO URGENT?

GOODNESS GRACIOUS!

HEY!
PLOP
SERI-OUSLY, WHAT ARE YOU DOING?!
DID YOU HEAR ME?!
SMOOCH
MN!
KISSS
MPH!
LICK
SMACK
HAH...
AH!
SLP
SMCH
HAH...

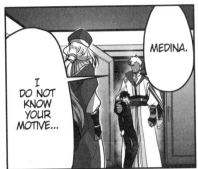

MEDINA.

I DO NOT KNOW YOUR MOTIVE...

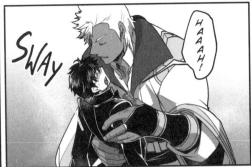

SWAY

HAAAH!

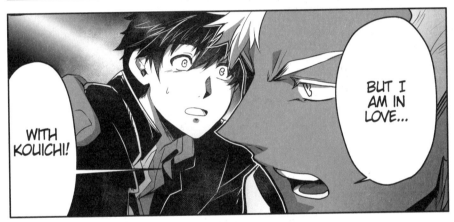

WITH KOUICHI!

BUT I AM IN LOVE...

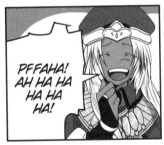

PFFAHA! AH HA HA HA HA HA!

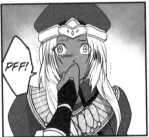

PFF!

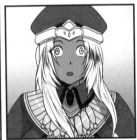

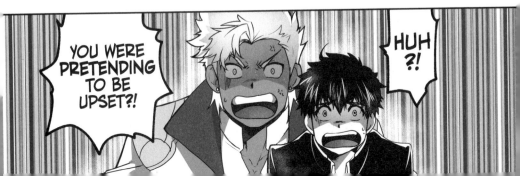

YOU WERE PRETENDING TO BE UPSET?!

HUH ?!

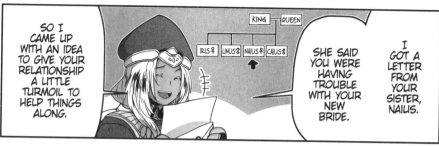

SO I CAME UP WITH AN IDEA TO GIVE YOUR RELATIONSHIP A LITTLE TURMOIL TO HELP THINGS ALONG.

KING — QUEEN
IRIS♀ | LINUS♂ | NAIUS♀ | CAIUS♂

SHE SAID YOU WERE HAVING TROUBLE WITH YOUR NEW BRIDE.

I GOT A LETTER FROM YOUR SISTER, NAIUS.

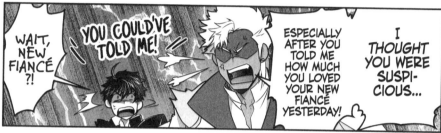

WAIT, NEW FIANCÉ?!

YOU COULD'VE TOLD ME!

ESPECIALLY AFTER YOU TOLD ME HOW MUCH YOU LOVED YOUR NEW FIANCÉ YESTERDAY!

I THOUGHT YOU WERE SUSPICIOUS...

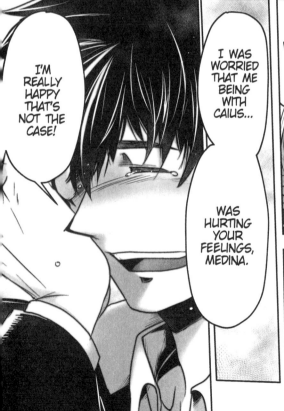

I'M REALLY HAPPY THAT'S NOT THE CASE!

I WAS WORRIED THAT ME BEING WITH CAIUS...

WAS HURTING YOUR FEELINGS, MEDINA.

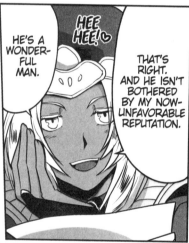

HE'S A WONDERFUL MAN.

HEE HEE!♡

THAT'S RIGHT. AND HE ISN'T BOTHERED BY MY NOW-UNFAVORABLE REPUTATION.

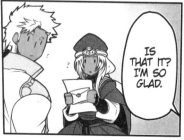

IS THAT IT? I'M SO GLAD.

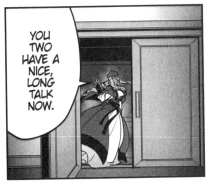

YOU TWO HAVE A NICE, LONG TALK NOW.

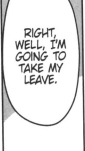

RIGHT, WELL, I'M GOING TO TAKE MY LEAVE.

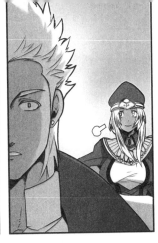

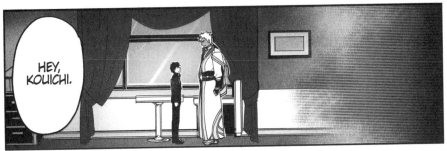

HEY, KOUICHI.

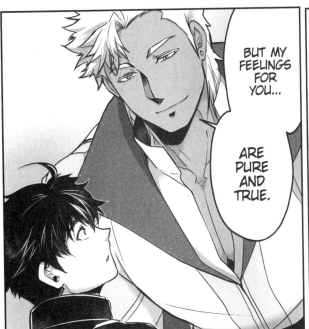

BUT MY FEELINGS FOR YOU...

ARE PURE AND TRUE.

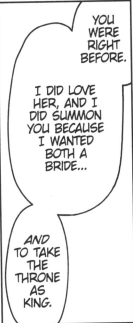

YOU WERE RIGHT BEFORE.

I DID LOVE HER, AND I DID SUMMON YOU BECAUSE I WANTED BOTH A BRIDE...

AND TO TAKE THE THRONE AS KING.

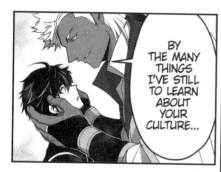

BY THE MANY THINGS I'VE STILL TO LEARN ABOUT YOUR CULTURE...

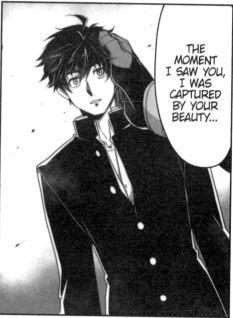

THE MOMENT I SAW YOU, I WAS CAPTURED BY YOUR BEAUTY...

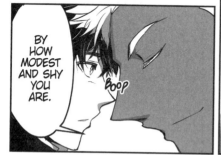

BY HOW MODEST AND SHY YOU ARE.

BOOP

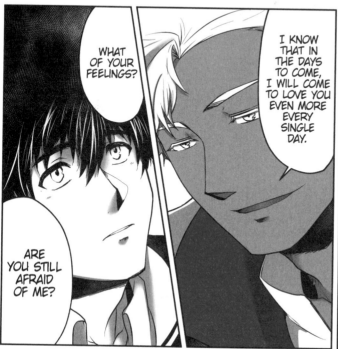

WHAT OF YOUR FEELINGS?

ARE YOU STILL AFRAID OF ME?

I KNOW THAT IN THE DAYS TO COME, I WILL COME TO LOVE YOU EVEN MORE EVERY SINGLE DAY.

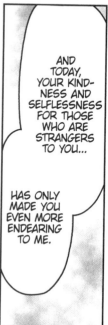

AND TODAY, YOUR KIND-NESS AND SELFLESSNESS FOR THOSE WHO ARE STRANGERS TO YOU...

HAS ONLY MADE YOU EVEN MORE ENDEARING TO ME.

……
I...
MN!
AH!
HAAH!
SQLCH
SQLCH
HAH!
SQLCH
GH!
SQLCH
SQLCH
AH!
SQLCH
ARE YOU ALL RIGHT?
SQLCH
QUIVER QUIVER
TWITCH
SQLCH
SQLCH
SQLCH
SQLCH
HAH!
HAAH!
YEAH... MN!
AH!
THAT'S TWO FINGERS.
SQLCH
SQLCH
AH, AH...!
THRUST
SQLCH
THRUST
SQLCH
DON'T RUB... DON'T RUB ME THERE ...!
JOLT
DON'T ...!

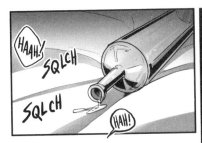

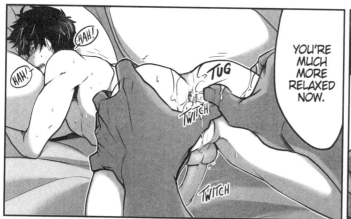

HAH! HAH!

TUG

TWITCH

TWITCH

YOU'RE MUCH MORE RELAXED NOW.

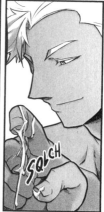

SQLCH

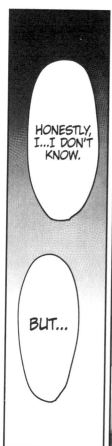

HONESTLY, I...I DON'T KNOW.

BUT...

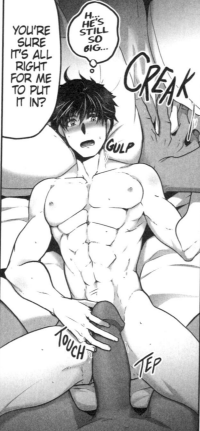

YOU'RE SURE IT'S ALL RIGHT FOR ME TO PUT IT IN?

H... HE'S STILL SO BIG...

GULP

CREAK

TOUCH

TEP

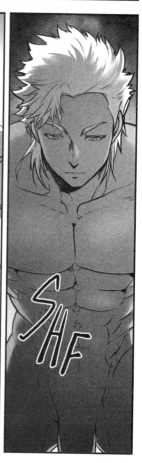

SHF

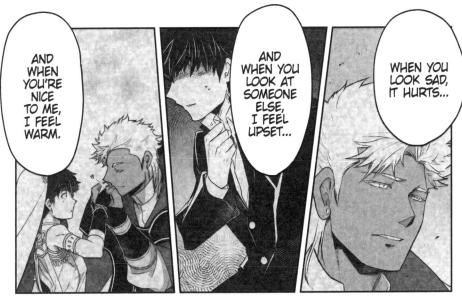

AND WHEN YOU'RE NICE TO ME, I FEEL WARM.

AND WHEN YOU LOOK AT SOMEONE ELSE, I FEEL UPSET...

WHEN YOU LOOK SAD, IT HURTS...

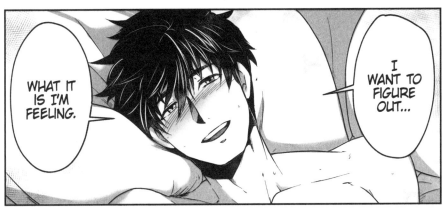

WHAT IT IS I'M FEELING.

I WANT TO FIGURE OUT...

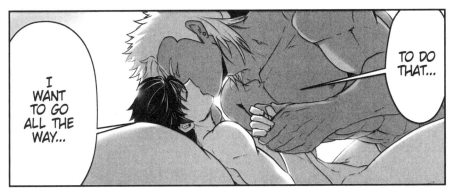

I WANT TO GO ALL THE WAY...

TO DO THAT...

HAH...
TWITCH
AH...
SHUDDER
GWAH...
SQLCH
SQLCH
PLP
TWITCH
AH... AH...
JOLT
ZLP
SQLCH
SQLCH
TWITCH
AHH...!!

AWWWW! YOU'RE SO LITTLE AND CUTE!
MEDINA, STOP!
YOUR CHEST... YOUR CHEST IS RIGHT IN MY FACE!
I'M SORRY, KOUICHI!
I WANTED TO DO THIS THE MOMENT I SAW YOU!
BWOMP
SQUEEEZE

......
JEALOUS MUCH?

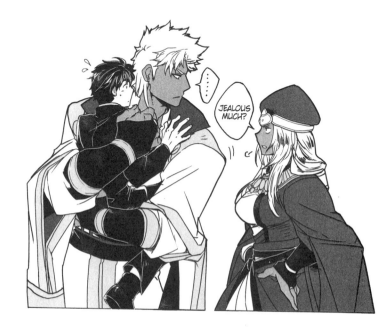

Chapter 4

AH...
TWITCH
TWITCH
HAH...
SQLCH
SQLCH
HAH!
HUFF!
I KNOW IT'S JUST THE TIP...
HAH!
HAH!
HUFF!
TREMBLE TREMBLE
BUT HE'S REALLY INSIDE ME...
SQLCH
TREMBLE TREMBLE TREMBLE
CAIUS IS INSIDE ME...
DOING ALL RIGHT, KOUICHI?
LET'S LET YOU ADJUST TO JUST THIS.
TELL ME IF IT'S TOO MUCH.
NOD
CREAK
MMKAY ...
TENSE

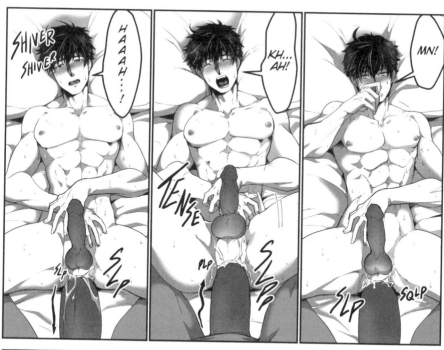

SHIVER
SHIVER

HAAAH....!

SLP
SLP

KH... AH!

TENSE

PLP

SLPP

MN!

SLP

SQLP

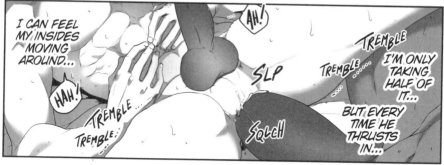

I CAN FEEL MY INSIDES MOVING AROUND...

AH!

HAH!

TREMBLE
TREMBLE...

SLP

SQLCH

TREMBLE

TREMBLE

I'M ONLY TAKING HALF OF IT...

BUT EVERY TIME HE THRUSTS IN...

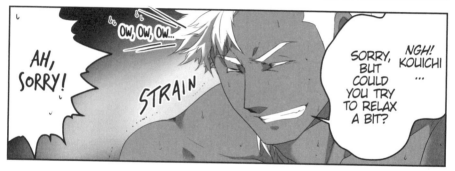

OW, OW, OW...

AH, SORRY!

STRAIN

NGH! KOUICHI...

SORRY, BUT COULD YOU TRY TO RELAX A BIT?

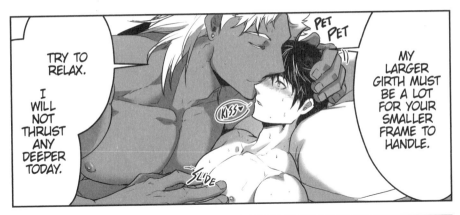

TRY TO RELAX.

I WILL NOT THRUST ANY DEEPER TODAY.

PET PET

KISS~

SLIDE

MY LARGER GIRTH MUST BE A LOT FOR YOUR SMALLER FRAME TO HANDLE.

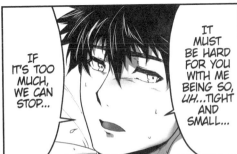

IF IT'S TOO MUCH, WE CAN STOP...

IT MUST BE HARD FOR YOU WITH ME BEING SO, UH...TIGHT AND SMALL...

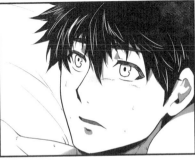

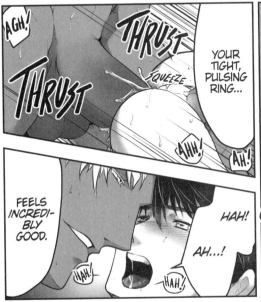

AGH!

THRUST

THRUST

SQUEEZE

YOUR TIGHT, PULSING RING...

AHH!

AH!

FEELS INCREDI-BLY GOOD.

HAH!

HAH!

AH...!

HAH!

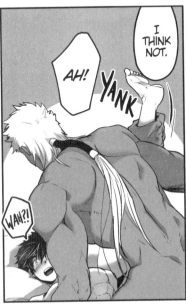

I THINK NOT.

AH!

YANK

WAH?!

HYAH!
AH...!
WAIT--!
THRUST
THRUST
SQLCH
SQLCH
SQLCH
SQLCH
TWITCH♥
THRUST
CREAK
CREAK
BUT MOST OF ALL...
OUR BODIES ARE CONNECTED.
N...
HOLY SHIT.
THAT'S ONLY HALF OF HIM? IT FEELS SO INCREDIBLE ALREADY!
AH...!
I COULDN'T BE HAPPIER.
THRUST
HAH!
AH!
THRUST
THRUST
AGH!
CREAK
CREAK

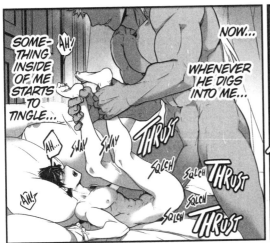

SOMETHING INSIDE OF ME STARTS TO TINGLE...

AH!

AH...

SWAY SWAY

AH...!

THRUST

SQLCH

SQLCH SQLCH

SQLCH

THRUST

THRUST

THRUST

NOW...

WHENEVER HE DIGS INTO ME...

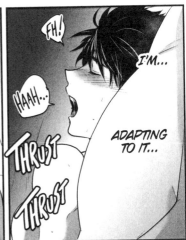

FH!

HAAH...

I'M...

ADAPTING TO IT...

THRUST

THRUST

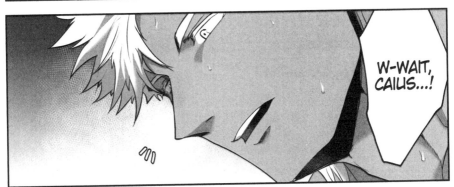

W-WAIT, CAIUS...!

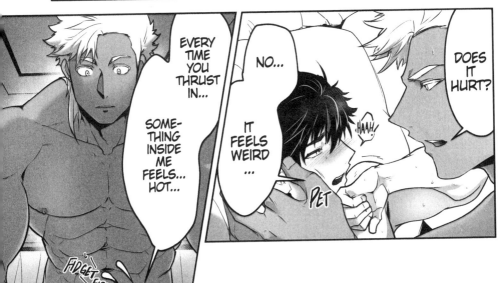

EVERY TIME YOU THRUST IN...

SOMETHING INSIDE ME FEELS... HOT...

NO...

IT FEELS WEIRD...

HAAH!

PET

DOES IT HURT?

FIDGET FIDGET

KOUICHI ...
THAT MEANS IT FEELS GOOD.
TUG
SLPP
CHUCKLE
WAH?!
HYAH ...?!
IT FEELS GOOD...?
HAH!
HUFF!
AH!
CREAK
AH...
CREAK
AH!
SQLCH
SQLCH
CREAK
SQLCH
CREAK
SQLCH
CREAK
CREAK
CREAK
GASP
GASP
I CAN'T BELIEVE IT...
I USED TO BE SO SCARED OF THIS HUGE TITAN...
LOOM...
SOB
SOB
FLINCH
AH!
AH!
BUT I WAS THE ONE WHO ASKED CAIUS TO FUCK ME, AND...
THRUST
HAH!
THRUST
THRUST
HAH!

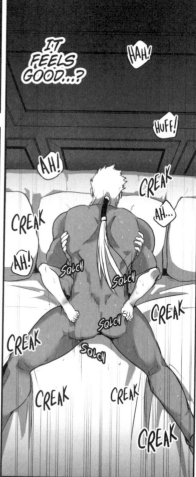

AH!
FHH...
FH!
HAAH!
THRUST
THRUST
IT FEELS GOOD!
SWAY
SWAY
SQLCH
THRUST
SQLCH
SQLCH
SQLCH
CAIUS ...!
CAIUS ...!
HUFF...
HUFF...
SWAY
SQLCH
SQLCH
SQLCH
SQLCH
AH!
CREAK
AHH!
SWAY
SWAY
AH!
AH!
CREAK
CREAK
I HEAR IT IN YOUR VOICE ...
YOU'RE CLOSE, AREN'T YOU?
AH!
HAH!
NO...
THRUST
THRUST
STROKE
STROKE
STROKE
THRUST
SWAY
SQLCH
SQLCH
SQLCH
SQLCH
SQLCH
THRUST
SWAY
I WANT YOU TO CUM FOR ME.
THRUST
AH... I'M GONNA CUM...
CREAK
CREAK
I'M GONNA CUM FROM CAIUS JERKING ME OFF...
AND FUCKING MY ASS!
I LOVE YOU, KOU-ICHI.
M...

!
THROB
TWITCH
SPURT
SPURT
SQUEEZE
SQUEEZE
SQLCH
SQLCH
SQLCH
SQLCH
TWITCH
TWITCH
TWITCH
DRIP
PLOP
POP
TWITCH
TWITCH
FH...
FAP FAP
FAP
FAP

SLURP
MM!
TWITCH
SHUDDER
SHUDDER
SPURT
THIS IS CAILUS'S CUM...
HAH!
HAH!
HE CAME SO MUCH...
SQLCH
SLP
MY BELLY'S ON FIRE...
ONLY TEN DAYS LEFT...
ZZZ...
ZZZ...

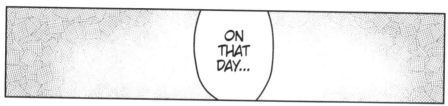

ON THAT DAY...

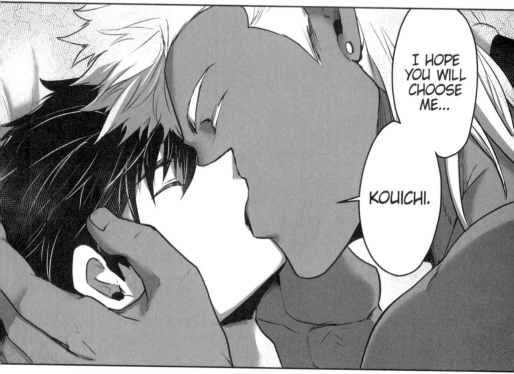

I HOPE YOU WILL CHOOSE ME...

KOUICHI.

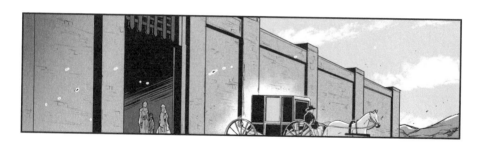

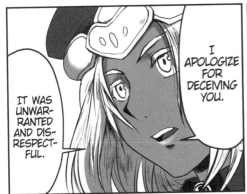
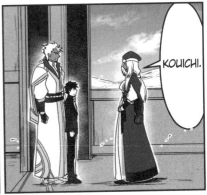

KOUICHI.

I APOLOGIZE FOR DECEIVING YOU.

IT WAS UNWARRANTED AND DISRESPECTFUL.

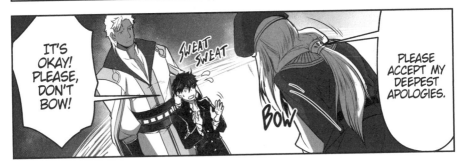

IT'S OKAY! PLEASE, DON'T BOW!

SWEAT SWEAT

BOW

PLEASE ACCEPT MY DEEPEST APOLOGIES.

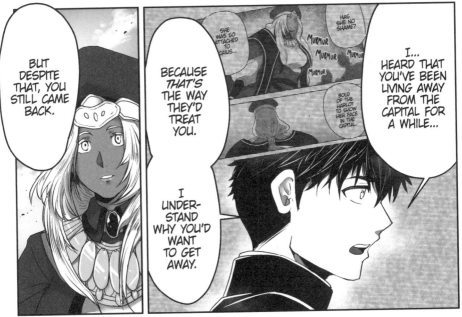

BUT DESPITE THAT, YOU STILL CAME BACK.

BECAUSE *THAT'S* THE WAY THEY'D TREAT YOU.

I UNDERSTAND WHY YOU'D WANT TO GET AWAY.

SHE WAS SO ATTACHED TO GAILIS...

MURMUR MURMUR MURMUR

MURMUR

HAS SHE NO SHAME?

BOLD OF THE HARLOT TO SHOW HER FACE IN THE CAPITAL

I... HEARD THAT YOU'VE BEEN LIVING AWAY FROM THE CAPITAL FOR A WHILE...

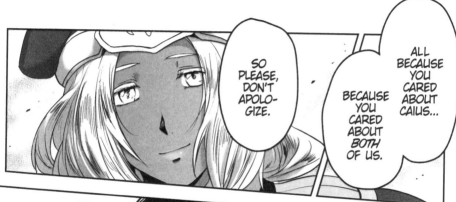

SO PLEASE, DON'T APOLO-GIZE.

ALL BECAUSE YOU CARED ABOUT CAIUS...

BECAUSE YOU CARED ABOUT *BOTH* OF US.

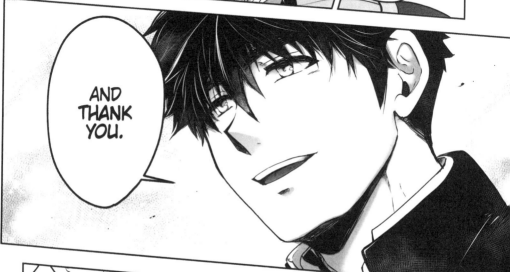

AND THANK YOU.

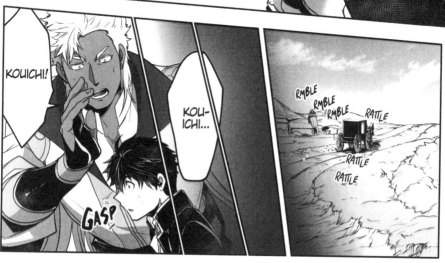

KOUICHI!

KOU-ICHI...

GASP

RMBLE

RMBLE

RMBLE

RATTLE

RATTLE

RATTLE

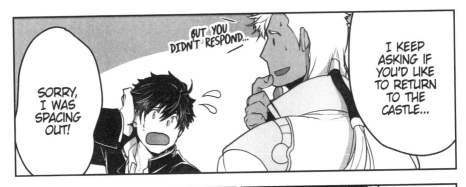

SORRY, I WAS SPACING OUT!

BUT YOU DIDN'T RESPOND...

I KEEP ASKING IF YOU'D LIKE TO RETURN TO THE CASTLE...

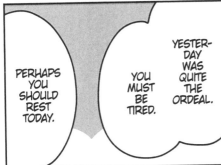

PERHAPS YOU SHOULD REST TODAY.

YOU MUST BE TIRED.

YESTER-DAY WAS QUITE THE ORDEAL.

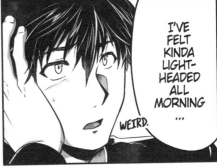

I'VE FELT KINDA LIGHT-HEADED ALL MORNING...

WEIRD.

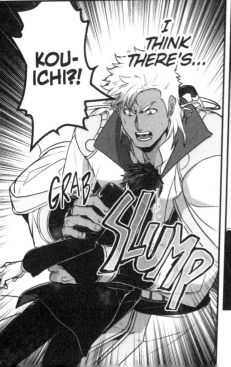

KOU-ICHI!?

I THINK THERE'S...

GRAB

SLUMP

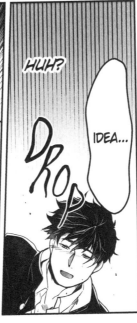

HUH?

IDEA...

DROP

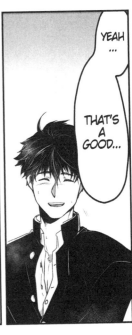

YEAH...

THAT'S A GOOD...

SOME-THING WRONG WITH ME...
IT'S OKAY, KOUICHI.
I'LL WORK HARD TO MAKE UP FOR DAD NOT BEING HERE.
DON'T YOU WORRY ABOUT A THING.
I'M DOING FINE. TOTALLY SETTLED IN.
I'LL BE FINE ON MY OWN, SO YOU GO GIVE 'EM HELL...
MOM.
HAH...
HAH...
HAH...
GH...
SHUDDER
HH...
I'M HOT...
IT HURTS...
FF...
HAH...
HAH...
GRIP
SHUDDER SHUDDER

HELP...
MOM...
HUFF!
HUFF!
I KNOW THERE'S NO POINT IN CALLING FOR THEM.
GRIP
DAD...
THEY'RE NOT THERE.
I'M ALONE.
SOME-ONE, HELP ME...
HAAH...
HAH!
ANY-ONE...
I'M...
KOUICHI!

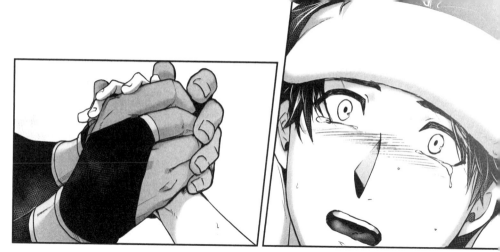

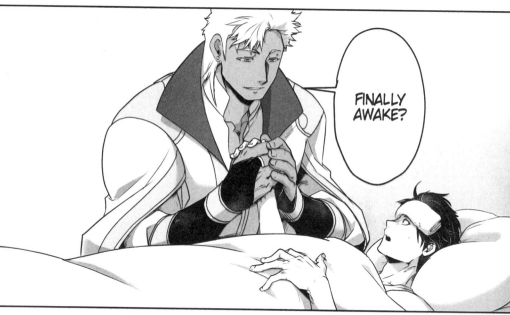

FINALLY AWAKE?

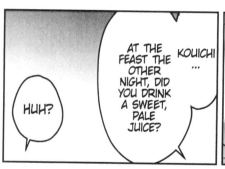

HUH?

AT THE FEAST THE OTHER NIGHT, DID YOU DRINK A SWEET, PALE JUICE?

KOUICHI...

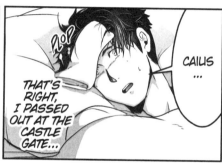

THAT'S RIGHT, I PASSED OUT AT THE CASTLE GATE...

CAIUS...

THAT JUICE WAS MADE FROM A KARINA FRUIT.

HONORABLE CONSORT.

I DID.

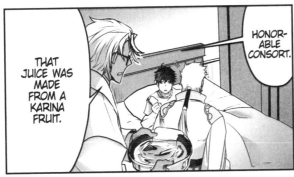

OH... YEAH.

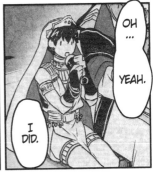

WHILE ITS JUICE IS INCREDIBLY DELICIOUS...

IT IS DEEPLY CONNECTED TO THE MAGIC POWER OF THE MOON.

THE KARINA FRUIT IS GROWN ONLY IN THE BEAST-MAN KINGDOM OF FOVAL.

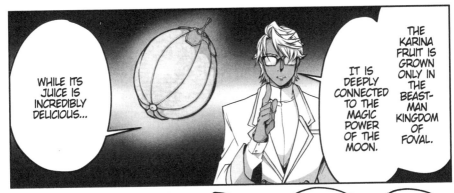

IT'S EXTREMELY DIFFICULT TO IMPORT, TOO.

WE RARELY HAVE KARINA FRUIT IN THE PALACE KITCHENS.

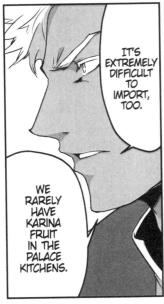

IS OTHERWISE *POISONOUS*.

WHILE HARMLESS TO LARGER, MORE STALWART RACES LIKE TITANS AND BEASTMEN...

IT CONTAINS POTENT COMPOUNDS THAT...

POISON-OUS...?!

SH OCK

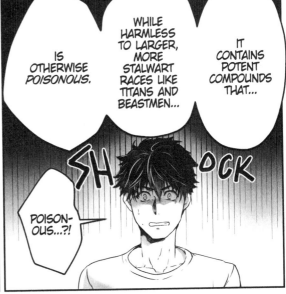

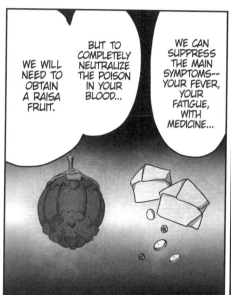

WE WILL NEED TO OBTAIN A RAISA FRUIT.

BUT TO COMPLETELY NEUTRALIZE THE POISON IN YOUR BLOOD...

WE CAN SUPPRESS THE MAIN SYMPTOMS-- YOUR FEVER, YOUR FATIGUE, WITH MEDICINE...

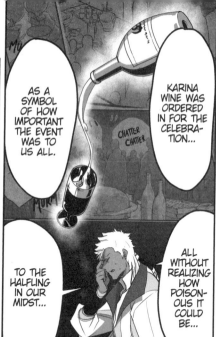

AS A SYMBOL OF HOW IMPORTANT THE EVENT WAS TO US ALL.

KARINA WINE WAS ORDERED IN FOR THE CELEBRA- TION...

TO THE HALFLING IN OUR MIDST...

ALL WITHOUT REALIZING HOW POISON- OUS IT COULD BE...

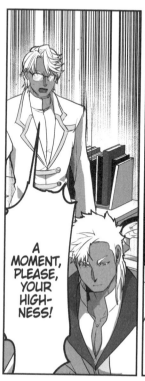

A MOMENT, PLEASE, YOUR HIGH- NESS!

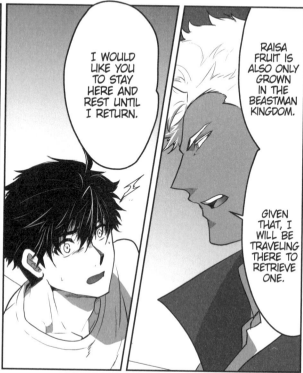

I WOULD LIKE YOU TO STAY HERE AND REST UNTIL I RETURN.

RAISA FRUIT IS ALSO ONLY GROWN IN THE BEASTMAN KINGDOM.

GIVEN THAT, I WILL BE TRAVELING THERE TO RETRIEVE ONE.

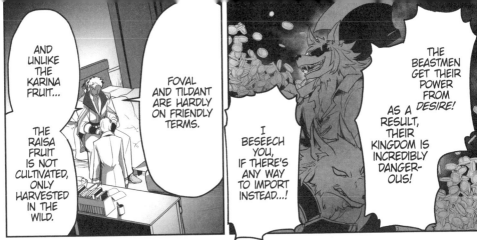

AND UNLIKE THE KARINA FRUIT...

THE RAISA FRUIT IS NOT CULTIVATED, ONLY HARVESTED IN THE WILD.

FOVAL AND TILDANT ARE HARDLY ON FRIENDLY TERMS.

I BESEECH YOU, IF THERE'S ANY WAY TO IMPORT INSTEAD...!

THE BEASTMEN GET THEIR POWER FROM *DESIRE!* AS A RESULT, THEIR KINGDOM IS INCREDIBLY DANGER-OUS!

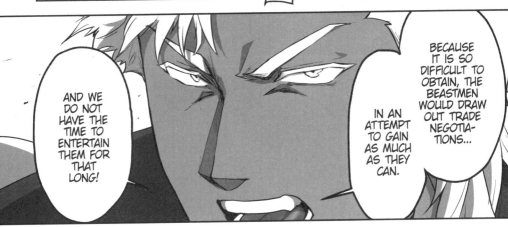

AND WE DO NOT HAVE THE TIME TO ENTERTAIN THEM FOR THAT LONG!

IN AN ATTEMPT TO GAIN AS MUCH AS THEY CAN.

BECAUSE IT IS SO DIFFICULT TO OBTAIN, THE BEASTMEN WOULD DRAW OUT TRADE NEGOTIA-TIONS...

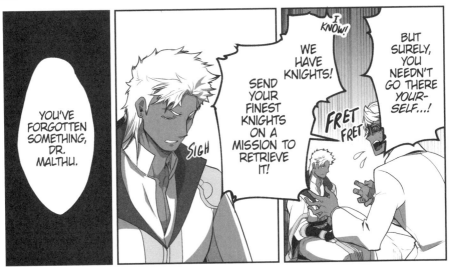

YOU'VE FORGOTTEN SOMETHING, DR. MALTHU.

SIGH

WE HAVE KNIGHTS! SEND YOUR FINEST KNIGHTS ON A MISSION TO RETRIEVE IT!

I KNOW!

FRET FRET

BUT SURELY, YOU NEEDN'T GO THERE YOUR-SELF...!

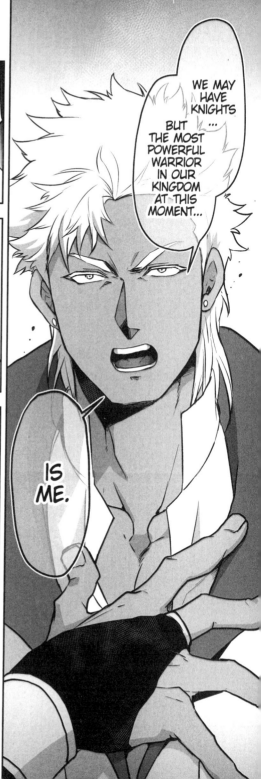

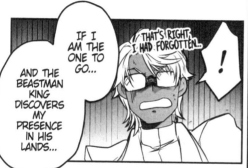

IF I AM THE ONE TO GO...

AND THE BEASTMAN KING DISCOVERS MY PRESENCE IN HIS LANDS...

THAT'S RIGHT, I HAD FORGOTTEN...

!

WE MAY HAVE KNIGHTS...

BUT THE MOST POWERFUL WARRIOR IN OUR KINGDOM AT THIS MOMENT...

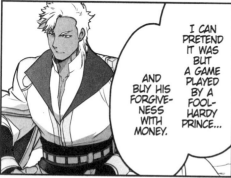

I CAN PRETEND IT WAS BUT A GAME PLAYED BY A FOOL-HARDY PRINCE...

AND BUY HIS FORGIVE-NESS WITH MONEY.

IS ME.

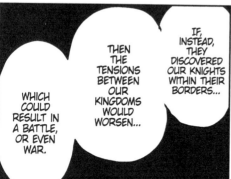

IF, INSTEAD, THEY DISCOVERED OUR KNIGHTS WITHIN THEIR BORDERS...

THEN THE TENSIONS BETWEEN OUR KINGDOMS WOULD WORSEN...

WHICH COULD RESULT IN A BATTLE, OR EVEN WAR.

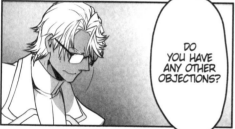

DO YOU HAVE ANY OTHER OBJECTIONS?

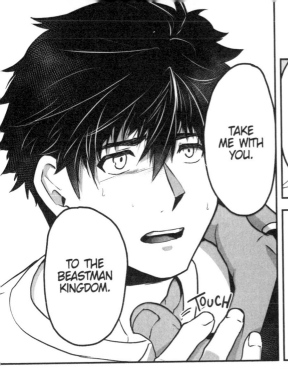

TAKE ME WITH YOU.

TO THE BEASTMAN KINGDOM.

=TOUCH

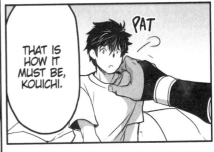

PAT

THAT IS HOW IT MUST BE, KOUICHI.

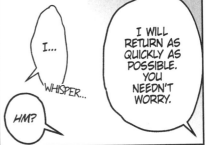

I...

WHISPER...

HM?

I WILL RETURN AS QUICKLY AS POSSIBLE. YOU NEEDN'T WORRY.

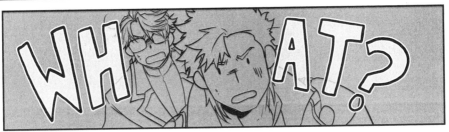

WH AT?

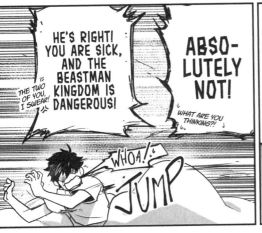

HE'S RIGHT! YOU ARE SICK, AND THE BEASTMAN KINGDOM IS DANGEROUS!

THE TWO OF YOU, I SWEAR!

ABSO- LUTELY NOT!

WHAT ARE YOU THINKING?!

WHOA!

JUMP

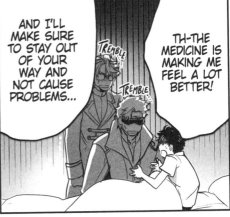

AND I'LL MAKE SURE TO STAY OUT OF YOUR WAY AND NOT CAUSE PROBLEMS...

TREMBLE

TREMBLE

TH-THE MEDICINE IS MAKING ME FEEL A LOT BETTER!

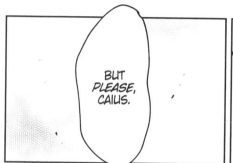

BUT PLEASE, CAIUS.

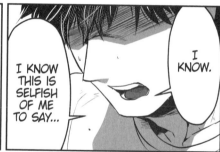

I KNOW THIS IS SELFISH OF ME TO SAY...

I KNOW.

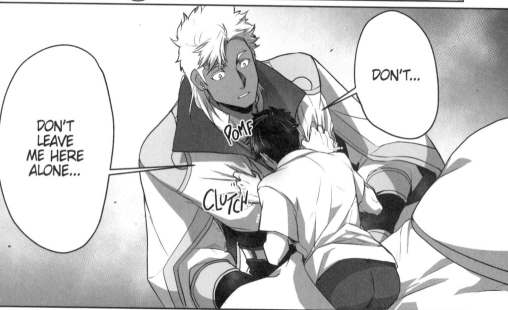

DON'T LEAVE ME HERE ALONE...

DON'T...

POMF

CLUTCH

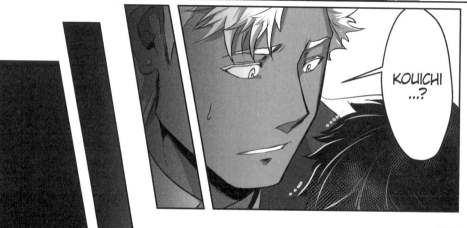

KOUICHI ...?

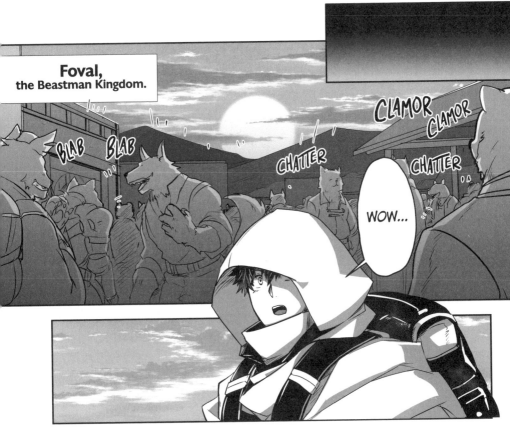

Foval,
the Beastman Kingdom.

BLAB BLAB

CHATTER

CLAMOR CLAMOR

CHATTER

WOW...

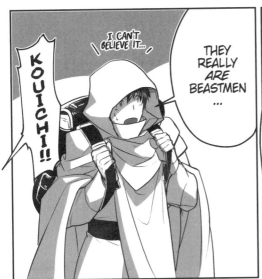

KOUICHI!!

I CAN'T BELIEVE IT...

THEY REALLY ARE BEASTMEN...

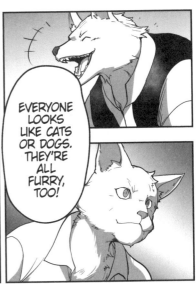

EVERYONE LOOKS LIKE CATS OR DOGS. THEY'RE ALL FURRY, TOO!

WE'VE ARRIVED FAR LATER THAN EXPECTED.
DASH
THE SUN IS SETTING. WE MUST HURRY!
GRAB
QUICKLY, TO OUR LODGINGS!
HUH? WAIT, WHY HURRY?!
WHAT'S THE RUSH?!
Your Highness.
There's one thing you should know about the karina poisoning.
There is one symptom the medicine cannot suppress.
You see...

IF WORD GOT OUT THAT WE'RE TRAVELING, IT COULD MEAN DISASTER. I'M COUNTING ON YOU TO COVER FOR US.
THANK YOU.
WHAT ?!

HAVE YOU SEEN THE PRINCE AND HIS BRIDE?
WHERE ARE THEY?
I...HEAR THEY'VE GONE OFF ON A LOVER'S RETREAT! GOODNESS, TALK ABOUT A LOVEY-DOVEY COUPLE!! AH HA HA!!!
A JOLT
TREMBLE

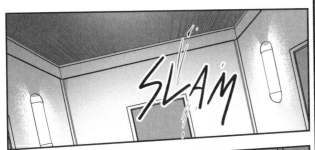

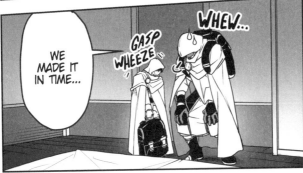

WE MADE IT IN TIME...

GASP WHEEZE

WHEW...

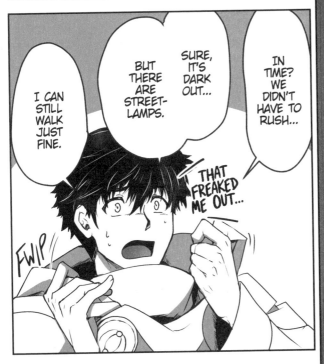

I CAN STILL WALK JUST FINE.

BUT THERE ARE STREET-LAMPS.

SURE, IT'S DARK OUT...

IN TIME? WE DIDN'T HAVE TO RUSH...

THAT FREAKED ME OUT...

FWIP

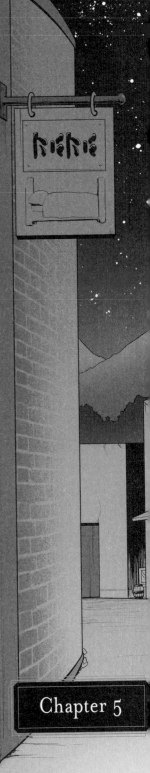

Chapter 5

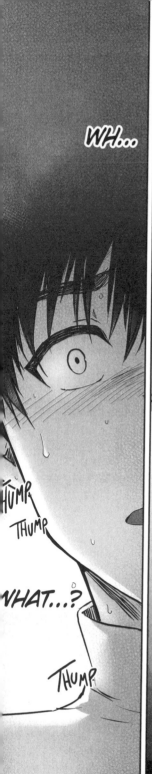

Wh...

THUMP
THUMP

WHAT...?

THUMP

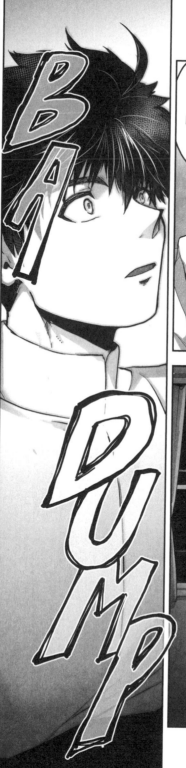

B
A

D
U
M
P

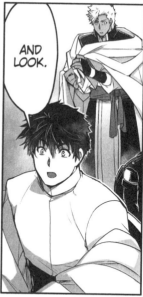

AND LOOK.

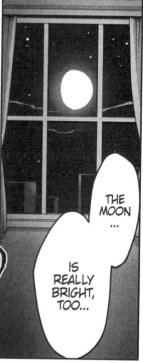

THE MOON ...

IS REALLY BRIGHT, TOO...

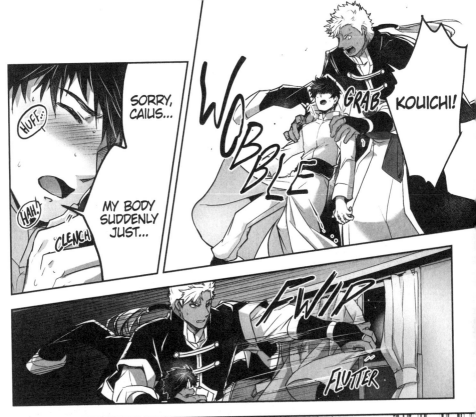

HUFF...

HAH...

CLENCH

SORRY, CAIUS...

MY BODY SUDDENLY JUST...

WOBBLE

GRAB

KOUICHI!

FWIP

FLUTTER

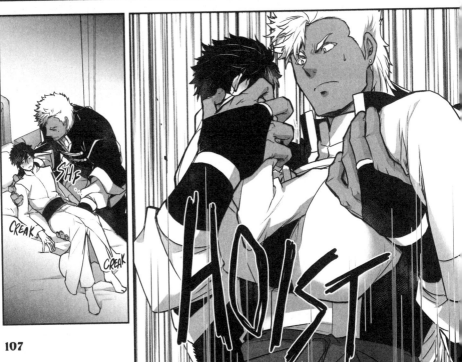

SHF

CREAK

CREAK

HOIST

THE KARINA FRUIT DRAWS POWER FROM THE MOON.

ITS POISON ALSO REACTS TO THE PRESENCE OF THE MOON.

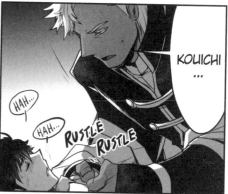

KOUICHI...

HAH...

HAH...

RUSTLE

RUSTLE

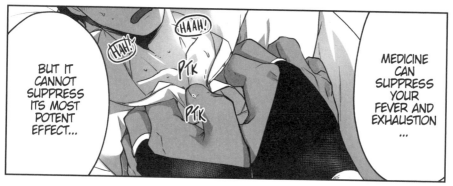

BUT IT CANNOT SUPPRESS ITS MOST POTENT EFFECT...

HAAH!

HAH!

PTK

PTK

MEDICINE CAN SUPPRESS YOUR FEVER AND EXHAUSTION...

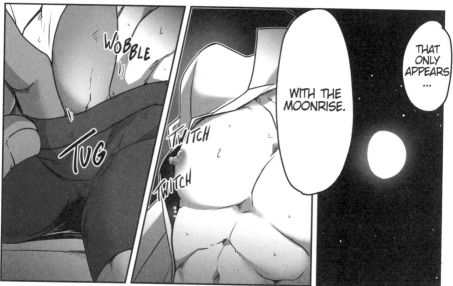

WOBBLE

TUG

TWITCH

TWITCH

WITH THE MOONRISE.

THAT ONLY APPEARS...

A RUSH OF AROUSAL.
AH...
AH!
JOLT
STROKE
STROKE
WAIT ...!
YOU'LL FEEL BETTER ONCE IT'S RELIEVED.
AH! AH...
GWAH! AH...
MY WHOLE BODY... IS SO SENSITIVE!
JOLT
HAH!
HAAH!
STROKE
STROKE
SHP
STROKE
SHLP
TWITCH
SHP
TWITCH
SHUDDER

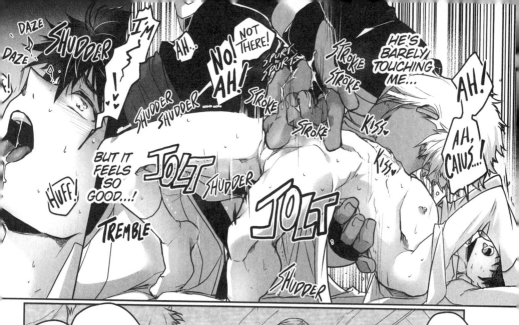

DAZE ♪
DAZE ♪
SHUDDER!
HUFF!

I'M

AH...

NO! NOT THERE! AH!

SPURT SPURT

SHUDDER SHUDDER
STROKE

STROKE
STROKE

HE'S BARELY TOUCHING ME...

KISS ♪

KISS ♪

AH!

AA, CAIUS...!

BUT IT FEELS SO GOOD...!

JOLT

SHUDDER

STROKE

TREMBLE

JOLT

SHUDDER

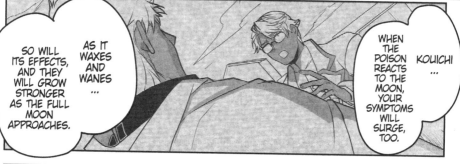

SO WILL ITS EFFECTS, AND THEY WILL GROW STRONGER AS THE FULL MOON APPROACHES.

AS IT WAXES AND WANES...

WHEN THE POISON REACTS TO THE MOON, YOUR SYMPTOMS WILL SURGE, TOO.

KOUICHI...

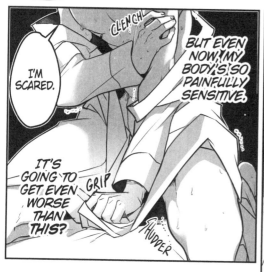

CLENCH!

I'M SCARED.

BUT EVEN NOW, MY BODY'S SO PAINFULLY SENSITIVE.

IT'S GOING TO GET EVEN WORSE THAN THIS?

GRIP

SHUDDER

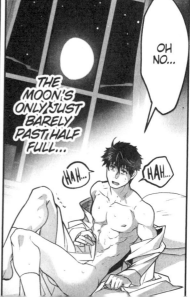

OH NO...

THE MOON'S ONLY JUST BARELY PAST HALF FULL...

HAH...

HAH...

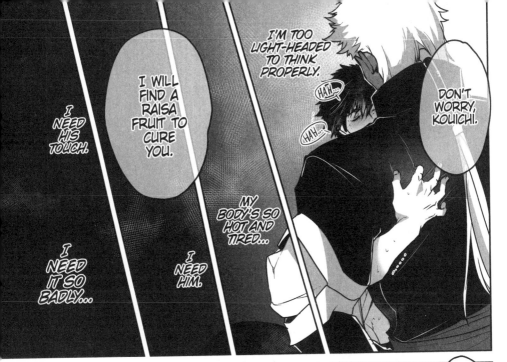

I NEED HIS TOUCH.

I WILL FIND A RAISA FRUIT TO CURE YOU.

I'M TOO LIGHT-HEADED TO THINK PROPERLY.

HAH...

HAH...

DON'T WORRY, KOUICHI.

MY BODY'S SO HOT AND TIRED...

I NEED IT SO BADLY...

I NEED HIM.

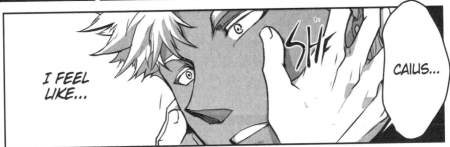

I FEEL LIKE...

SHF

CAIUS...

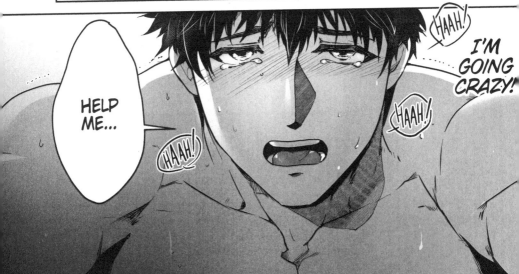

HELP ME...

HAAH!

HAAH!

HAAH!

I'M GOING CRAZY!

MN!
SLP
FH!
SLP
HAH!
SLP
SLRP
SLCH
HMNH!
CAILIS' COCK...
SLURP
LICK
MN!
TOUCH
NGH!
IT'S SO BIG...
...
NOM
MPH!
NPH...
MPH!
SUCK
I CAN'T EVEN FIT IT IN MY MOUTH.
SUCK
HE FUCKED ME WITH THIS HUGE COCK...
HAH!
SLP
SLRP
SHLP
MPH!
SLRP
SLP
SLP
TWITCH
TWITCH
NN!
SLP
TWITCH

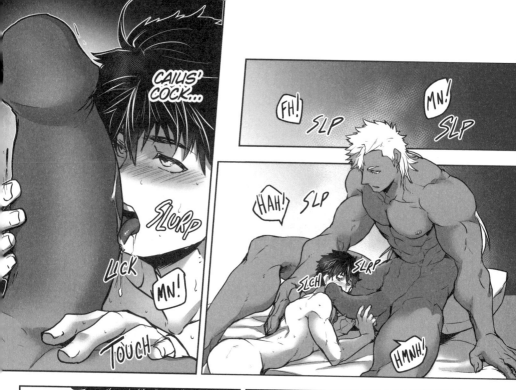

I'M SORRY, I'M NOT AS GOOD AS YOU ARE...
I CAN'T GET IT IN MY MOUTH...
COUGH COUGH
CHUCKLE
PLEASE.
YOUR EAGER STRUGGLING WAS ACTUALLY QUITE AROUSING TO WATCH.
AND WHILE I KNOW...
IT MAY BE THE POISON CAUSING YOU TO DESIRE ME SO BRAZENLY...
HAH!
AH!
YOUR FINGER- AH!
JOLT
HYAH!
RUB RUB
POKE
POKE
SLP
IT MAKES ME SO VERY HAPPY.
AH... AH!
YES, JUST LIKE THAT.
SLP
SQLCH
SQLCH
SHUDDER
LOWER YOUR HIPS, SLOWLY.
FH...
NGH!
HAH!
HAH!
SLIDE
SQLCH
SQLCH

HAH... AH!
SHUDDER
CLENCH
AH...
HAH!
PET PET
HAH!
PAT PAT
IT'S... IN...!
THAT HUGE COCK...
SQLCH
SQLCH
IT'S ALL THE WAY INSIDE ME!
SHUDDER
SHUDDER
SQLCH
SQLCH
MAYBE IT'S THE KARINA FRUIT, BUT IT DOESN'T HURT AT ALL...
HAH!
IN FACT...
HAH!
THAT'S IT. MOVE YOUR HIPS, DO WHAT WILL MAKE YOU FEEL GOOD.
CREAK
SOMETHING INSIDE OF ME KEEPS ACHING FOR MORE...
GH... AH!♥
THRUST
AH!
HAH!
HAH!
THRUST
YES...
CREAK
IT FEELS SO GOOD...!
HAH!..
SLP
THRUST
THRUST
SLP
SLP
SQLCH
SLP
SQLCH
SQLCH
THAT'S GOOD.
CREAK
CREAK

AH, NO!
LICK
NOT THERE, IT'S... HAH... AH!
TWITCH
WRAP
NOM
TWITCH
OH, GOD...
THRUST
SLP
SLP
NO!
THRUST
AH!
THRUST
THRUST
GWAH!
HIS HUGE TONGUE...
NO!
FLICK
IS PLAYING WITH MY NIPPLE.
FLICK
HAH!
HIS HUGE COCK...
AH!
THRUST
SWING
SWING
AHN!
SQLCH
SQLCH
IS HITTING DEEP INSIDE ME...
SQLCH
THRUST
THRUST
IT'S... AMAZING... AH!♥
THRUST
IT FEELS SO GOOD.
THRUST
I CAN'T STOP FUCKING HIM...!
SQLCH
SQLCH
SLP
SHCK
SHCK
THRUST
THRUST
THRUST
AAAHH!♥

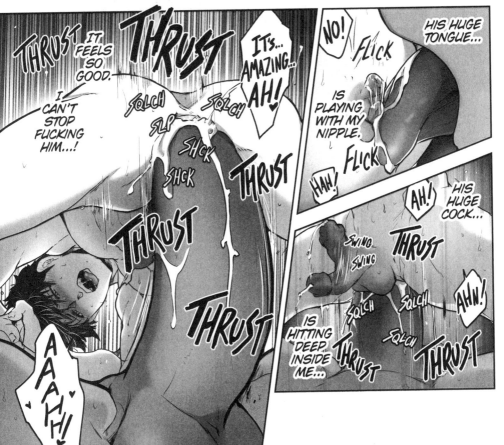

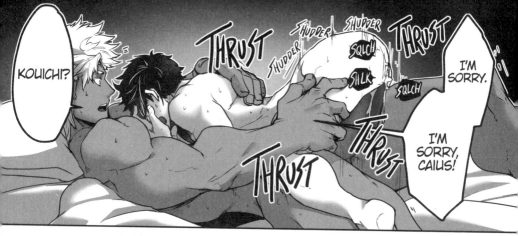

KOUICHI?

THRUST

SHUDDER SHUDDER SHUDDER

THRUST

SHUDDER

SQLCH

SILK

SQLCH

I'M SORRY.

I'M SORRY, CAIUS!

THRUST

THRUST

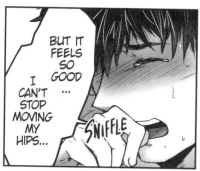

BUT IT FEELS SO GOOD...

I CAN'T STOP MOVING MY HIPS...

SNIFFLE

BECAUSE I'M SHY AND MODEST...

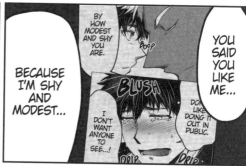

BY HOW MODEST AND SHY YOU ARE.

POOP

BLUSH

I DON'T WANT ANYONE TO SEE...!

DRIP

DRIP

DON'T LIKE DOING IT OUT IN PUBLIC.

YOU SAID YOU LIKE ME...

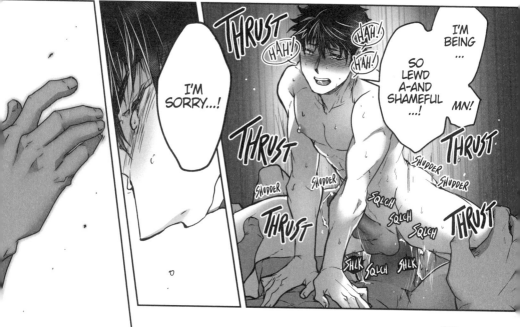

THRUST

HAH!

HAH!

HAH!

HAH!

I'M SORRY...!

I'M BEING...

SO LEWD A-AND SHAMEFUL...!

MN!

THRUST

SHUDDER

SHUDDER

SHUDDER

SHUDDER

THRUST

SQLCH

SQLCH

THRUST

SQLCH

SHLK

SQLCH

SHLK

THRUST

YOU HAVE NOTHING TO BE ASHAMED OF.
THERE'S NO SHAME IN SEEKING PLEASURE.
WHETHER YOU'RE SHY...
OR SHAMELESSLY PURSUING ME...
I FIND YOU COMPLETELY CAPTIVATING.

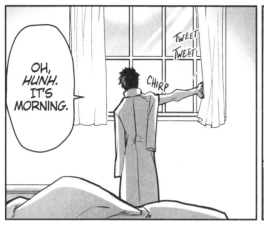

OH, HUNH. IT'S MORNING.

CHIRP

TWEET TWEET

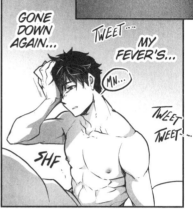

GONE DOWN AGAIN...

MY FEVER'S...

TWEET...

MN...

TWEET TWEET...

SHF

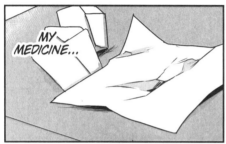

MY MEDICINE...

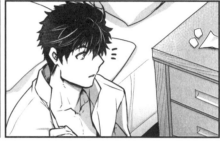

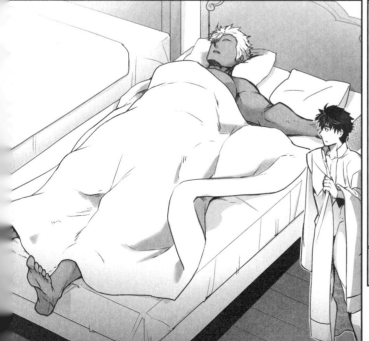

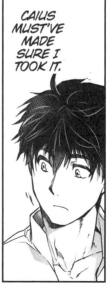

CAIUS MUST'VE MADE SURE I TOOK IT.

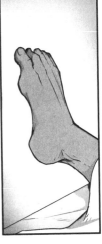

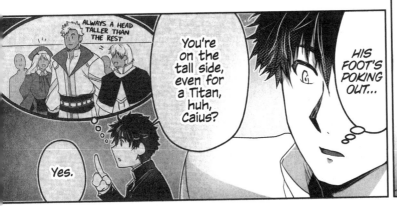

ALWAYS A HEAD TALLER THAN THE REST

You're on the tall side, even for a Titan, huh, Caius?

HIS FOOT'S POKING OUT...

Yes.

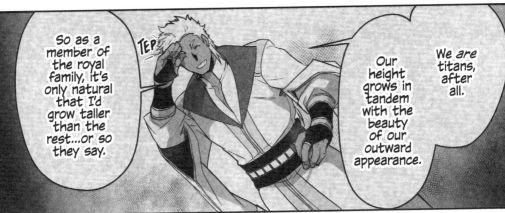

TEP

So as a member of the royal family, it's only natural that I'd grow taller than the rest...or so they say.

Our height grows in tandem with the beauty of our outward appearance.

We are titans, after all.

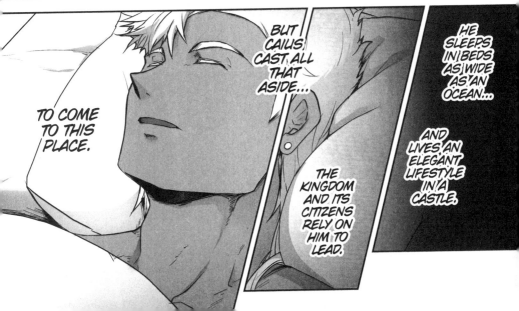

BUT CAIUS CAST ALL THAT ASIDE...

HE SLEEPS IN BEDS AS WIDE AS AN OCEAN...

TO COME TO THIS PLACE.

THE KINGDOM AND ITS CITIZENS RELY ON HIM TO LEAD.

AND LIVES AN ELEGANT LIFESTYLE IN A CASTLE.

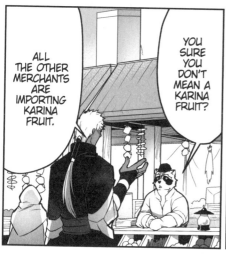

ALL THE OTHER MERCHANTS ARE IMPORTING KARINA FRUIT.

YOU SURE YOU DON'T MEAN A KARINA FRUIT?

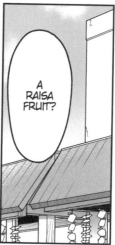

A RAISA FRUIT?

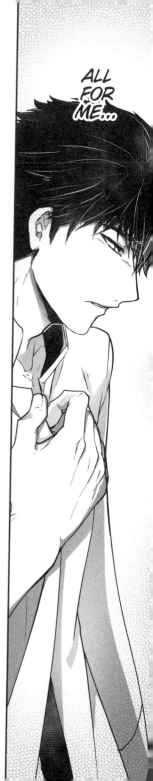

ALL FOR ME...

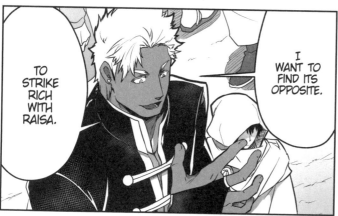

TO STRIKE RICH WITH RAISA.

I WANT TO FIND ITS OPPOSITE.

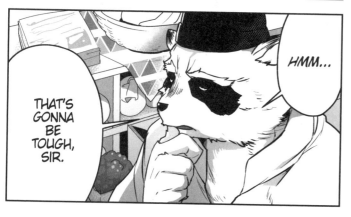

THAT'S GONNA BE TOUGH, SIR.

HMM...

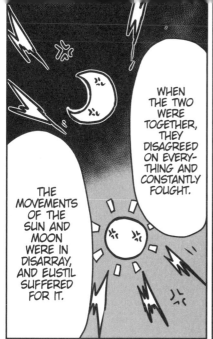

WHEN THE TWO WERE TOGETHER, THEY DISAGREED ON EVERYTHING AND CONSTANTLY FOUGHT.

THE MOVEMENTS OF THE SUN AND MOON WERE IN DISARRAY, AND EUSTIL SUFFERED FOR IT.

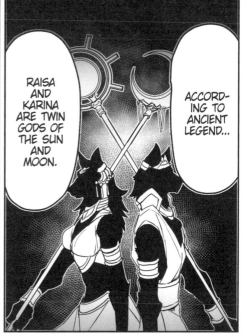

RAISA AND KARINA ARE TWIN GODS OF THE SUN AND MOON.

ACCORDING TO ANCIENT LEGEND...

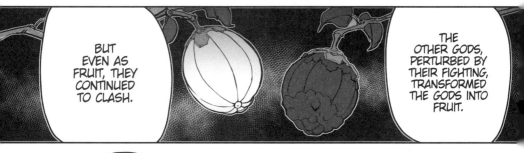

BUT EVEN AS FRUIT, THEY CONTINUED TO CLASH.

THE OTHER GODS, PERTURBED BY THEIR FIGHTING, TRANSFORMED THE GODS INTO FRUIT.

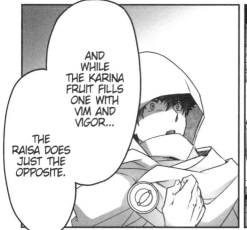

AND WHILE THE KARINA FRUIT FILLS ONE WITH VIM AND VIGOR...

THE RAISA DOES JUST THE OPPOSITE.

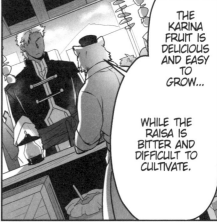

THE KARINA FRUIT IS DELICIOUS AND EASY TO GROW...

WHILE THE RAISA IS BITTER AND DIFFICULT TO CULTIVATE.

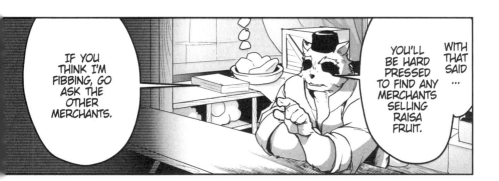

IF YOU THINK I'M FIBBING, GO ASK THE OTHER MERCHANTS.

WITH THAT SAID...

YOU'LL BE HARD PRESSED TO FIND ANY MERCHANTS SELLING RAISA FRUIT.

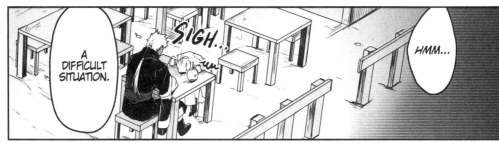

A DIFFICULT SITUATION.

SIGH...

HMM...

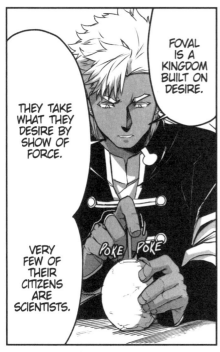

FOVAL IS A KINGDOM BUILT ON DESIRE.

THEY TAKE WHAT THEY DESIRE BY SHOW OF FORCE.

VERY FEW OF THEIR CITIZENS ARE SCIENTISTS.

POKE POKE

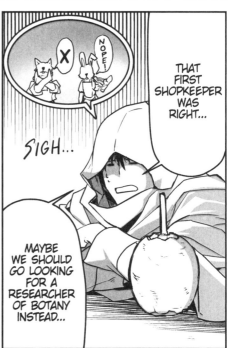

X

NOPE!

SIGH...

THAT FIRST SHOPKEEPER WAS RIGHT...

MAYBE WE SHOULD GO LOOKING FOR A RESEARCHER OF BOTANY INSTEAD...

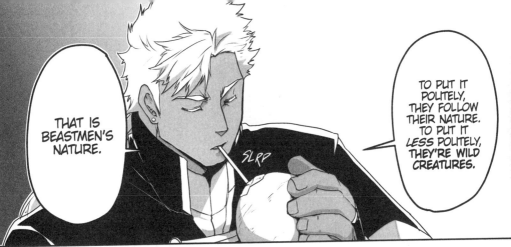

THAT IS BEASTMEN'S NATURE.

TO PUT IT POLITELY, THEY FOLLOW THEIR NATURE. TO PUT IT LESS POLITELY, THEY'RE WILD CREATURES.

SLRP

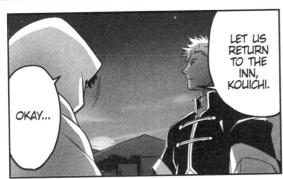

LET US RETURN TO THE INN, KOUICHI.

OKAY...

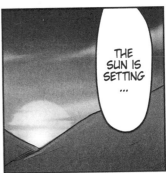

THE SUN IS SETTING ...

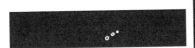

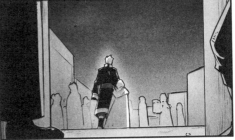

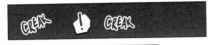

CREAK   CREAK

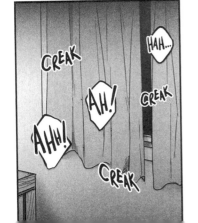

CREAK

HAH...

AH!

CREAK

AHH!

CREAK

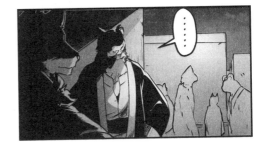

· · · · · ·

AGHHHH!
TWITCH
TWITCH
TWITCH
TWITCH
THRUST
THRUST
SPURT
THRUST
SQLCH
SQLCH
DID YOU CUM AGAIN?
HUFF...
HUFF!
CHUCKLE
THAT'S THE THIRD TIME TONIGHT.
I'M SORRY ...
I CAN'T HOLD BACK...
FH!
SNIFFLE
I DON'T WANT YOU TO.
CREAK
AH!
AH!
HAH!
HAH!
CREAK
AH!
NO!
THRUST
SLAP
SLAP
HAH!
CREAK
CREAK
THRUST
CREAK
CREAK
THRUST
HAH!

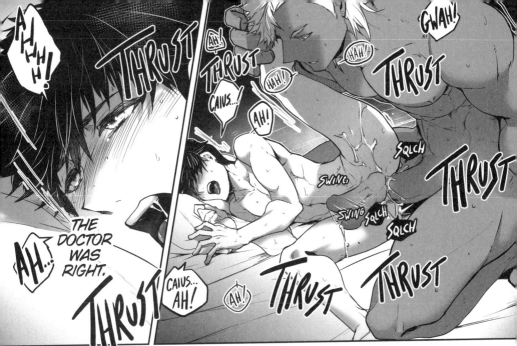

THE DOCTOR WAS RIGHT.

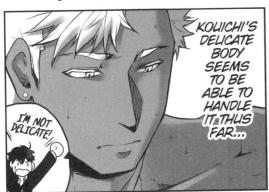

KOUICHI'S DELICATE BODY SEEMS TO BE ABLE TO HANDLE IT THUS FAR...

I'M NOT DELICATE!

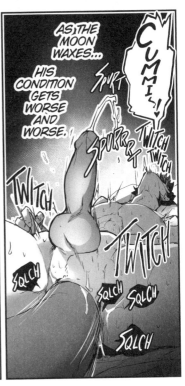

AS THE MOON WAXES... HIS CONDITION GETS WORSE AND WORSE.

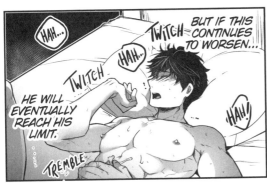

HAH...

HAH...

BUT IF THIS CONTINUES TO WORSEN...

HE WILL EVENTUALLY REACH HIS LIMIT.

I NEED TO FIND A RAISA FRUIT, QUICKLY...

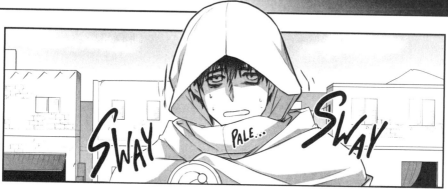

SWAY

PALE...

SWAY

I WANT TO STAY WITH YOU.

KOUICHI, YOU CAN REST UP AT THE INN.

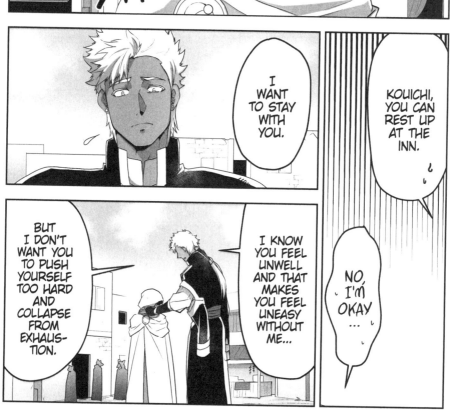

BUT I DON'T WANT YOU TO PUSH YOURSELF TOO HARD AND COLLAPSE FROM EXHAUSTION.

I KNOW YOU FEEL UNWELL AND THAT MAKES YOU FEEL UNEASY WITHOUT ME...

NO, I'M OKAY...

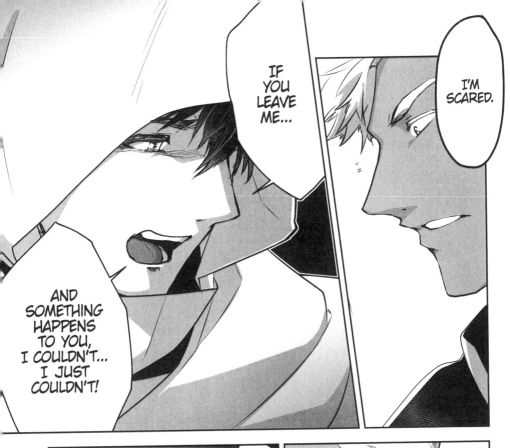

IF YOU LEAVE ME...

I'M SCARED.

AND SOMETHING HAPPENS TO YOU, I COULDN'T... I JUST COULDN'T!

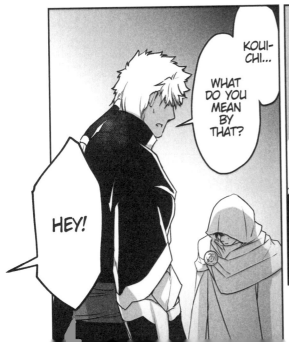

KOUI-CHI...

WHAT DO YOU MEAN BY THAT?

HEY!

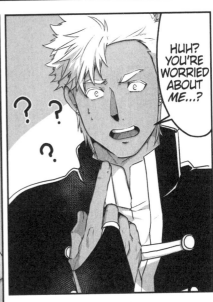

HUH? YOU'RE WORRIED ABOUT ME...?

TRYING TO FIND A MERCHANT SELLIN' RAISA FRUIT?

YOU THE GUYS...

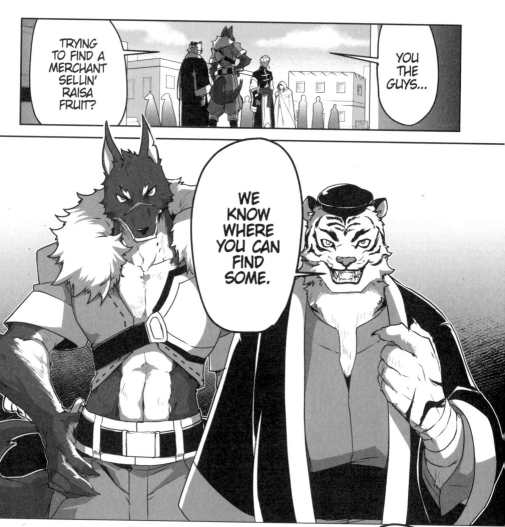

WE KNOW WHERE YOU CAN FIND SOME.

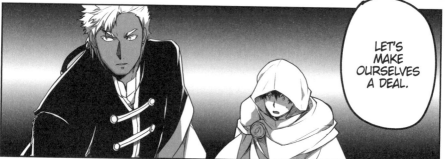

LET'S MAKE OURSELVES A DEAL.

THESE TWO LOOK SUSPICIOUS...
A TIGER!
IT'S A TIGER!
GRIP

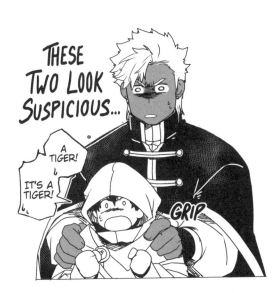

WE'RE NOT SUSPICIOUS!
NOT AT ALL!

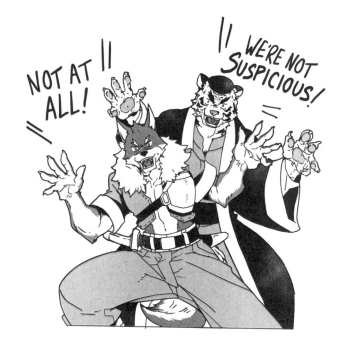

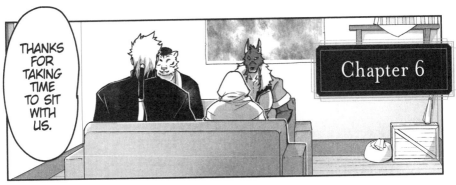

THANKS FOR TAKING TIME TO SIT WITH US.

Chapter 6

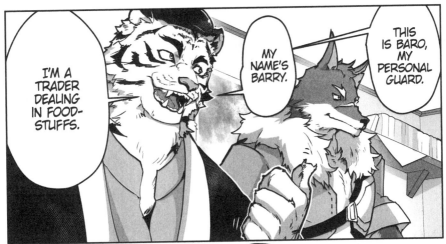

I'M A TRADER DEALING IN FOOD-STUFFS.

MY NAME'S BARRY.

THIS IS BARO, MY PERSONAL GUARD.

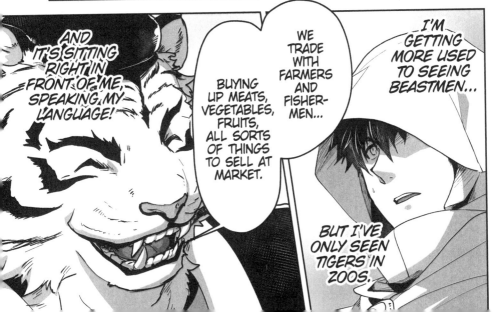

AND IT'S SITTING RIGHT IN FRONT OF ME, SPEAKING MY LANGUAGE!

WE TRADE WITH FARMERS AND FISHER-MEN...

BUYING UP MEATS, VEGETABLES, FRUITS, ALL SORTS OF THINGS TO SELL AT MARKET.

I'M GETTING MORE USED TO SEEING BEASTMEN...

BUT I'VE ONLY SEEN TIGERS IN ZOOS.

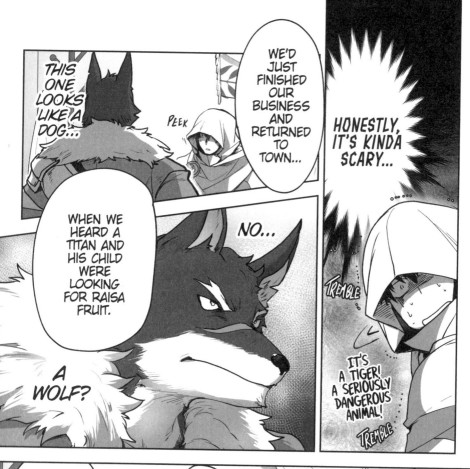

THIS ONE LOOKS LIKE A DOG...

PEEK

WE'D JUST FINISHED OUR BUSINESS AND RETURNED TO TOWN...

HONESTLY, IT'S KINDA SCARY...

WHEN WE HEARD A TITAN AND HIS CHILD WERE LOOKING FOR RAISA FRUIT.

NO...

TREABLE

IT'S A TIGER! A SERIOUSLY DANGEROUS ANIMAL!

A WOLF?

TREMBLE

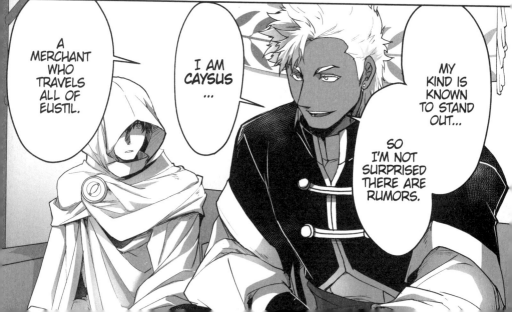

A MERCHANT WHO TRAVELS ALL OF EUSTIL.

I AM CAYSUS ...

MY KIND IS KNOWN TO STAND OUT...

SO I'M NOT SURPRISED THERE ARE RUMORS.

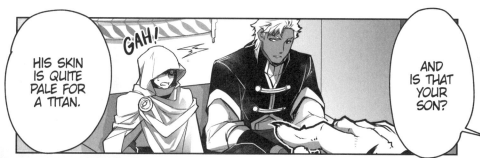

HIS SKIN IS QUITE PALE FOR A TITAN.

GAH!

AND IS THAT YOUR SON?

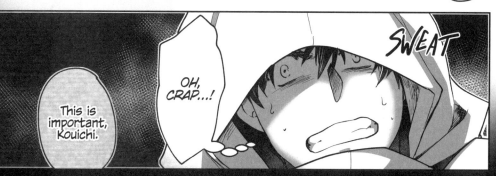

OH, CRAP...!

SWEAT

This is important, Kouichi.

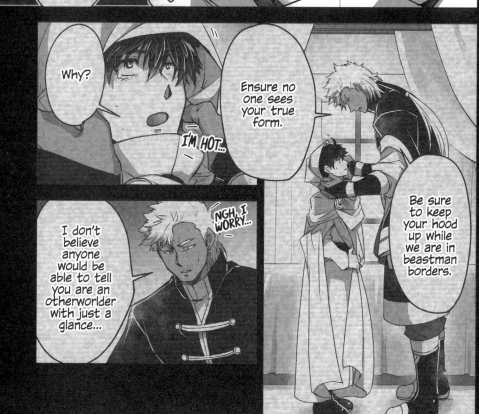

Why?

Ensure no one sees your true form.

I'M HOT...

Be sure to keep your hood up while we are in beastman borders.

NGH, I WORRY...

I don't believe anyone would be able to tell you are an otherworlder with just a glance...

halflings are a rare sight in Eustil.

but after a genocide long in the past...

FRANTIC

OH, CRAP, WHAT DO I SAY?

who knows what they would do.

If the desire-driven beastmen discover a halfling in their midst...

SADLY, SHE AND HER HUSBAND PASSED AWAY, SO I'VE TAKEN HIM IN.

HIS PALE SKIN RESULTS FROM HIS FATHER'S STRONG BLOOD...

TUG

THIS IS MY YOUNGER SISTER'S SON.

TMP

AS HE WAS A NORTH-ERN TITAN.

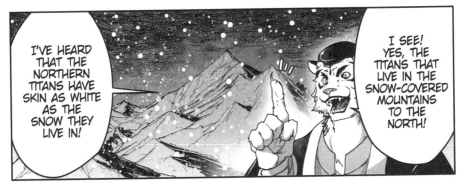

I'VE HEARD THAT THE NORTHERN TITANS HAVE SKIN AS WHITE AS THE SNOW THEY LIVE IN!

I SEE! YES, THE TITANS THAT LIVE IN THE SNOW-COVERED MOUNTAINS TO THE NORTH!

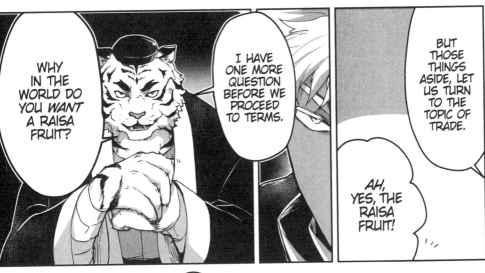

WHY IN THE WORLD DO YOU *WANT* A RAISA FRUIT?

I HAVE ONE MORE QUESTION BEFORE WE PROCEED TO TERMS.

BUT THOSE THINGS ASIDE, LET US TURN TO THE TOPIC OF TRADE.

AH, YES, THE RAISA FRUIT!

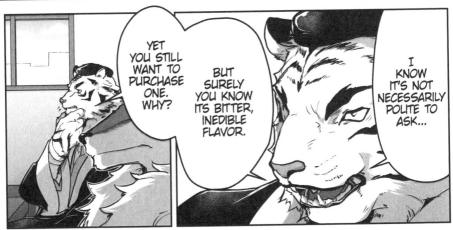

YET YOU STILL WANT TO PURCHASE ONE. WHY?

BUT SURELY YOU KNOW ITS BITTER, INEDIBLE FLAVOR.

I KNOW IT'S NOT NECESSARILY POLITE TO ASK...

IT ISN'T *JUST* BEAST-MEN...

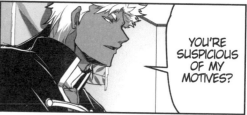

YOU'RE SUSPICIOUS OF MY MOTIVES?

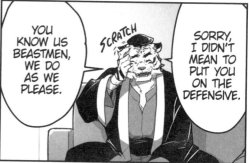

SORRY, I DIDN'T MEAN TO PUT YOU ON THE DEFENSIVE.

YOU KNOW US BEASTMEN, WE DO AS WE PLEASE.

SCRATCH

WHO HAVE THAT RELENTLESS, DECEITFUL DRIVE.

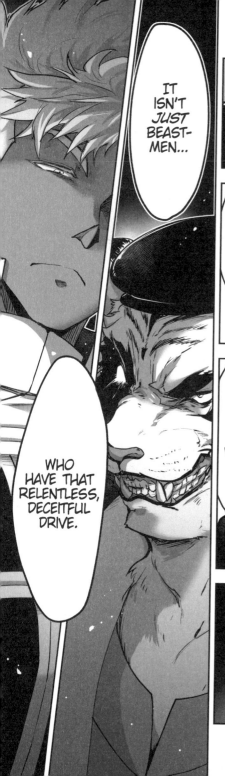

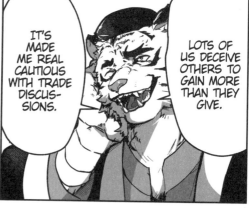

LOTS OF US DECEIVE OTHERS TO GAIN MORE THAN THEY GIVE.

IT'S MADE ME REAL CAUTIOUS WITH TRADE DISCUS-SIONS.

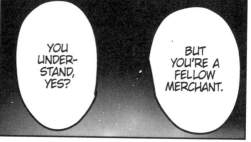

BUT YOU'RE A FELLOW MERCHANT.

YOU UNDER-STAND, YES?

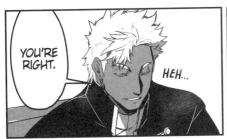

YOU'RE RIGHT.

HEH...

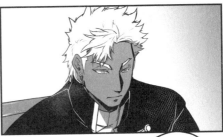

HE WANTS TO KNOW THE DELICIOUS TASTE OF A KARINA FRUIT.

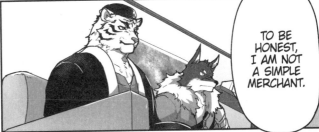

TO BE HONEST, I AM NOT A SIMPLE MERCHANT.

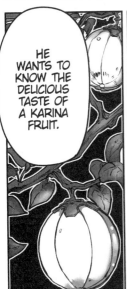

I'M A MERCENARY ON ASSIGNMENT FROM A RICH ELVEN NOBLEMAN.

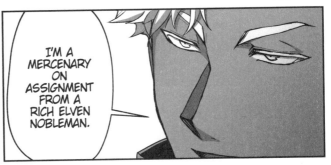

TO WARD OFF THOSE EFFECTS, HE WILL NEED A RAISA FRUIT.

HE WOULD INEVITABLY BE POISONED BY THE VERY FRUIT HE LUSTS AFTER.

HOWEVER, ELVES ARE LESS STALWART THAN TITANS AND BEASTMEN.

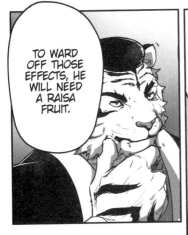

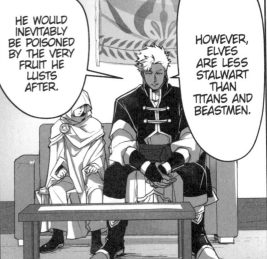

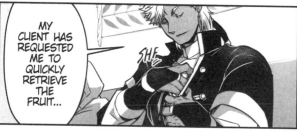

MY CLIENT HAS REQUESTED ME TO QUICKLY RETRIEVE THE FRUIT...

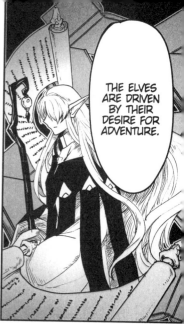

THE ELVES ARE DRIVEN BY THEIR DESIRE FOR ADVENTURE.

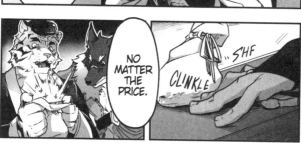

NO MATTER THE PRICE.

SHF

CLINKLE

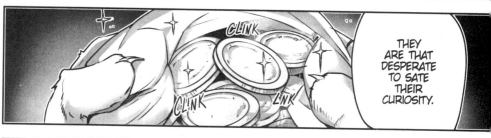

CLINK

CLINK

LNK

THEY ARE THAT DESPERATE TO SATE THEIR CURIOSITY.

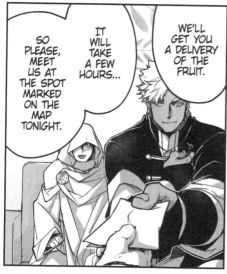

SO PLEASE, MEET US AT THE SPOT MARKED ON THE MAP TONIGHT.

IT WILL TAKE A FEW HOURS...

WE'LL GET YOU A DELIVERY OF THE FRUIT.

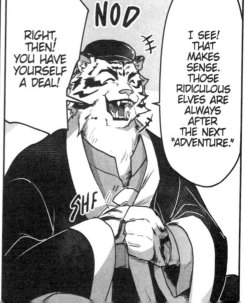

NOD

RIGHT, THEN! YOU HAVE YOURSELF A DEAL!

I SEE! THAT MAKES SENSE. THOSE RIDICULOUS ELVES ARE ALWAYS AFTER THE NEXT "ADVENTURE."

SHF

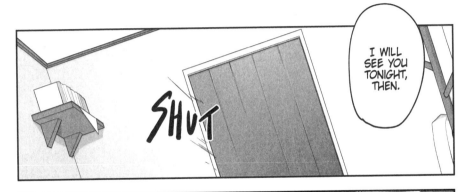

I WILL SEE YOU TONIGHT, THEN.

SHUT

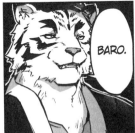

BARO.

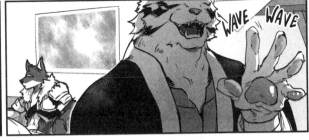

WAVE WAVE

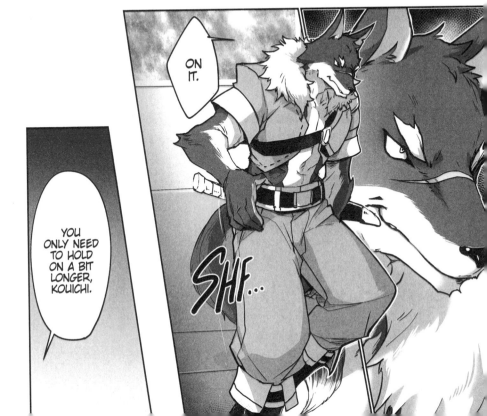

ON IT.

YOU ONLY NEED TO HOLD ON A BIT LONGER, KOUICHI.

SHF...

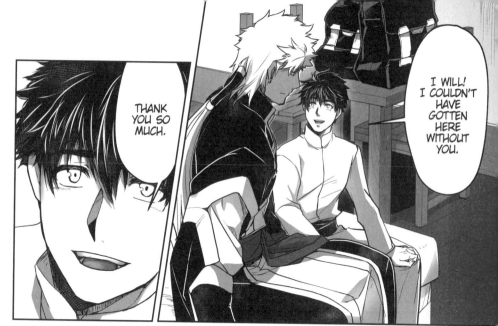

THANK YOU SO MUCH.

I WILL! I COULDN'T HAVE GOTTEN HERE WITHOUT YOU.

BUT WILL YOU WAIT FOR ME?

I KNOW IT WILL BE HARD ON YOUR BODY ALONE...

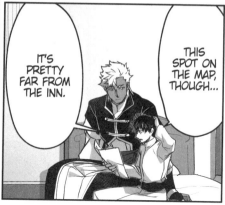

IT'S PRETTY FAR FROM THE INN.

THIS SPOT ON THE MAP, THOUGH...

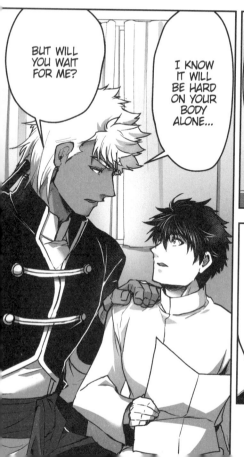

I CANNOT BRING YOU WITH ME, NOT TONIGHT.

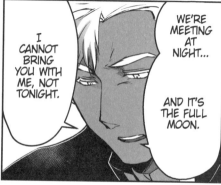

WE'RE MEETING AT NIGHT...

AND IT'S THE FULL MOON.

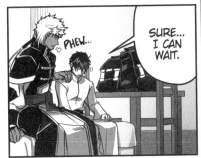

PHEW...

SURE... I CAN WAIT.

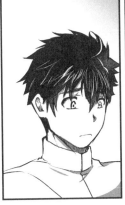

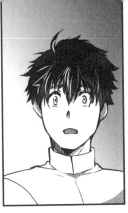

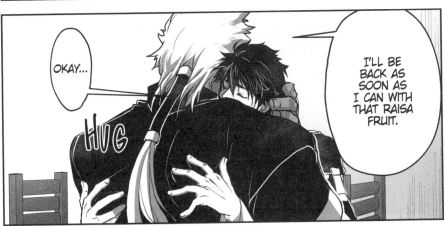

OKAY...

I'LL BE BACK AS SOON AS I CAN WITH THAT RAISA FRUIT.

HUG

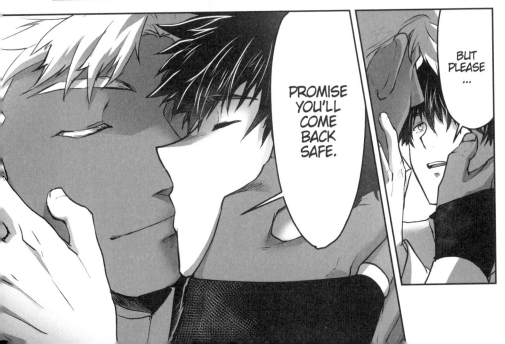

PROMISE YOU'LL COME BACK SAFE.

BUT PLEASE...

SQLCH
MN!
SQLCH
FH...
SQLCH
SQLCH
SQLCH
NGH...
SQLCH
SQLCH
SQLCH
HAH...
FH!
FH...
HAAH...
SQLCH
SQLCH
SQLCH
SQLCH
TWITCH
I'M SO HOT...
SO WORKED UP...
NGH!
SO FRUSTRAT-ED...
THIS ISN'T HELPING AT ALL...

HOLY CRAP... MY NIPPLES ARE SO HARD.
WHOA...
THEY'RE SO SENSITIVE...
TWITCH
TWITCH
TOUCH
I WANT HIM TO USE HIS BIG TONGUE...
TO LICK AND TEASE THEM!
I WANT HIM TO USE HIS STRONG FINGERS...
TO PINCH AND TWIST THEM!
GH-! AH!
HAH!
HAH!
AH...!
HAH!
RUB
SQLCH
RUB
SQLCH
SQLCH
SQLCH
TWITCH
TWITCH
IT'S NOT ENOUGH!
FH!
IT'S NOT NEARLY ENOUGH!
FH!

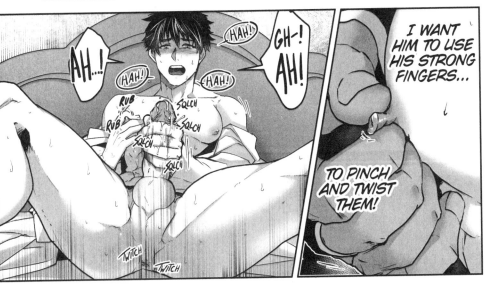

HAH!
I NEED HIM...
HAH!
SHF
PUSH
AH!
I NEED HIM...
TWITCH
I NEED CAIUS...
I NEED HIM TO FUCK ME!
SHUDDER
AHHH!
THRUST
SQLCH
TWITCH
TWITCH
AH!
SO...
GOOD ...!
SQLCH
SQLCH
SQLCH
SQLCH
TWITCH
TWITCH
SQLCH
TWITCH
SQLCH
AH!
HAAH!
AH...
SQLCH
SQLCH

CAIUS!
SQLCH
SQLCH
SQLCH
HAH!
CAIUS ...!
HAH!
WOW... I...
I CAN'T BELIEVE HOW I'VE CHANGED...
BEFORE, I'D JACK OFF...
WHILE I THOUGHT ABOUT FUCKING GIRLS.
HAAH
HAAH
SQUEEZE
FAP
FAP
FAP
FAP
NOW...
I'M FANTASIZING ABOUT GETTING FUCKED...
LICK
TWITCH
WRAP
TWITCH
THRUST
SLP
SLP
THRUST
THRUST
THRUST
AH!
HAH!
AGH!
AND JACKING OFF TO THE THOUGHT!
SQLCH
SQLCH
SQLCH
TWITCH
I WANT YOUR COCK ...!
THRUST
THRUST
THRUST
THRUST
HAH... AH... CAIUS, I WANT...
TWITCH
SLP
SLP
SLP

I NEED MORE ...
RUB
SQLCH
AH!
FUCK ME DEEPER ...!
HAH!
SQLCH
SQLCH
SQLCH
I WANT CAIUS TO FUCK ME.
I WANT HIM TO CALL MY NAME IN THAT SWEET VOICE...
I WANT HIM TO FILL ME TO THE BRIM...
WITH HIS HUGE COCK!
I WANT HIM TO DESTROY MY ASS!
SQLCH
TWITCH
SQLCH
SQLCH
AH!
HAH!
FH!
TWITCH
SQLCH
SQLCH
SQLCH
SQLCH
SLP
SLP
SLP
SLP
SQLCH
SQLCH
I WANT HIM TO FUCK ME HARD AND FAST!
MN!
MNN!

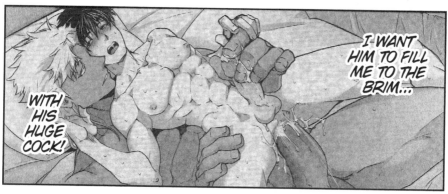

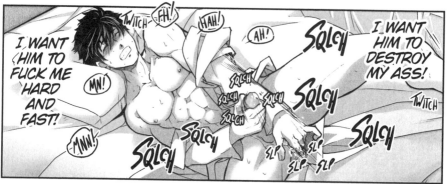

AS DEEP AS HE CAN GO...!
SHUDDER
TWITCH
AH... I'M CUM-MING!
I'M CUMMING, I'M CUMMING!
AH... AHHH~!
TWITCH
TWITCH
SPLURT
SPURT
SLP
SLP
TENSE
TWITCH
SLP
SLP
HAH...
HAH...
HAH...
FH...
TWITCH
TWITCH
HAH...
MN...!
TWITCH
FH...
FH!
HAH!
AH!
SLP
SLP
SLK

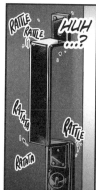

RATTLE RATTLE

HUH...?

RATTLE

RATATA

RATTLE

RATATA

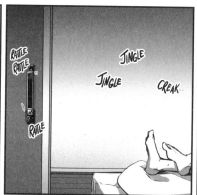

RATTLE RATTLE

RATTLE

JINGLE

JINGLE

CREAK

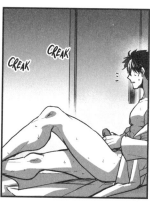

CREAK

CREAK

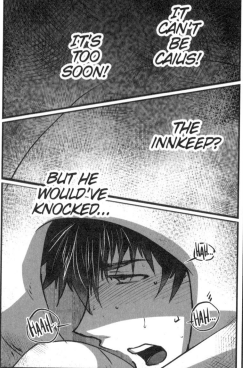

IT'S TOO SOON!

IT CAN'T BE CAIUS!

THE INNKEEP?

BUT HE WOULD'VE KNOCKED...

HAH...

HAAH...

HAH...

SHUDDER

S...

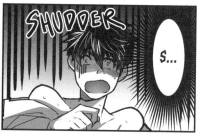

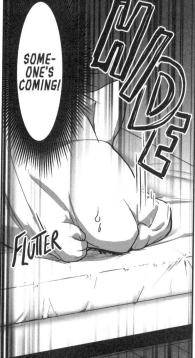

SOME-ONE'S COMING!

HIDE

FLUTTER

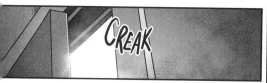

CREAK

CREAK
IT'S THAT BEASTMAN FROM THIS AFTER-NOON!
WHAT IS HE DOING HERE?
WHAT'S HE LOOKING FOR...?
SNEAK
SNEAK
CREAK
GRAB
HOIST
HOIST
?!
WHAP
CLENCH
TH--

THIEF!
LEAP
URGH!
WHUMP!!
YOU LITTLE BRAT! I THOUGHT YOU WERE ASLEEP!
DROP OUR BAGS!
KICK
KICK
STRAIN
TCH!
YOU SHOULD'VE ...
GRAB
STAYED IN BED!
WHAM
AGH!!
WHUNK

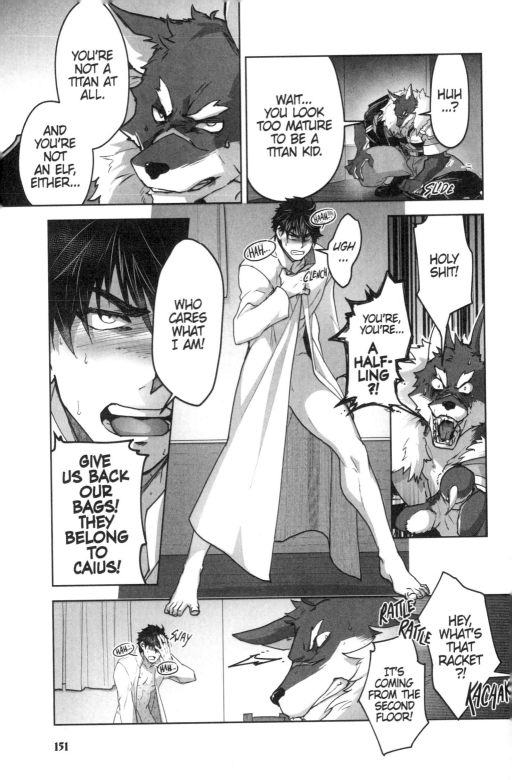

YOU'RE NOT A TITAN AT ALL.

AND YOU'RE NOT AN ELF, EITHER...

WAIT... YOU LOOK TOO MATURE TO BE A TITAN KID.

HUH ...?

SLIDE

HAAH......

HAH...

UGH ...

CLENCH

WHO CARES WHAT I AM!

HOLY SHIT!

YOU'RE, YOU'RE... A HALF-LING ?!

GIVE US BACK OUR BAGS! THEY BELONG TO CAIUS!

HAH...

SWAY

HAH...

RATTLE RATTLE

HEY, WHAT'S THAT RACKET ?!

IT'S COMING FROM THE SECOND FLOOR!

KACHAK

C'MON, SQUIRT!
IF YOU DON'T WANNA GET HURT...
KEEP YOUR HEAD DOWN!
GASP
WHAM
SHATTER
CLINKLE
CLINKLE
SHF
GRAB
SHATTER
CRACKLE
CLINK

CAIUS
...!
WHOOOOSH

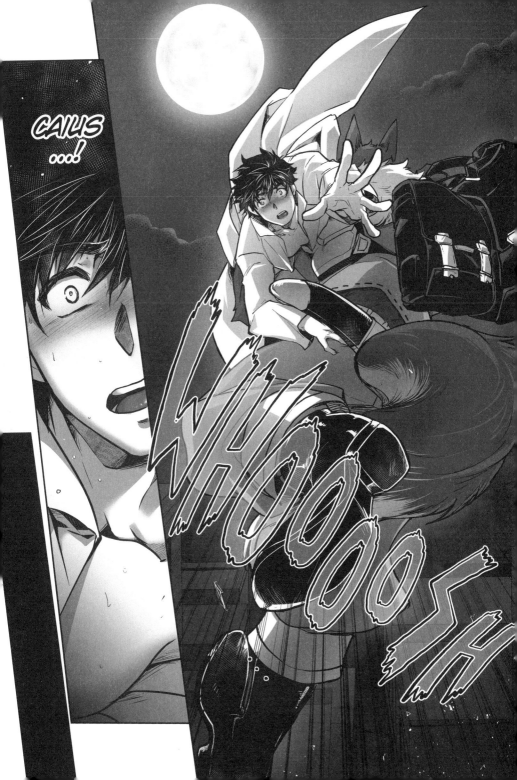

NO SUDDEN MOVES, NOW.
YOU TITANS MIGHT BE STRONG AS ALL HELL...
BUT YOU CAN'T TAKE ON ALL OF US AT ONCE.

Volume 1 : END

THE
TITAN'S
BRIDE

THE
TITAN'S
BRIDE

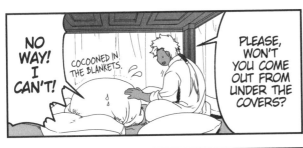

NO WAY! I CAN'T!

COCOONED IN THE BLANKETS.

PLEASE, WON'T YOU COME OUT FROM UNDER THE COVERS?

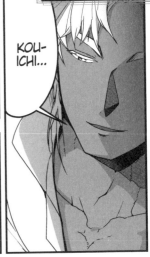

KOU-ICHI...

I DON'T KNOW HOW I'M GONNA BE ABLE TO LOOK YOU IN THE EYE!

THRUST

TREMBLE TREMBLE

JUST REMEMBERING WHAT WE DID YESTERDAY MAKES ME WANNA DIE FROM EMBARRASS-MENT...

※CHAPTER 4

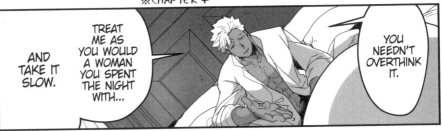

AND TAKE IT SLOW.

TREAT ME AS YOU WOULD A WOMAN YOU SPENT THE NIGHT WITH...

YOU NEEDN'T OVERTHINK IT.

ACK! HEY!

TUG

WHAT ?!

I WAS A VIRGIN! IN EVERY SENSE OF THE WORD!

HOW AM I SUP-POSED TO DO THAT WHEN I'VE NEVER EVEN SLEPT WITH A WOMAN, EITHER ?!

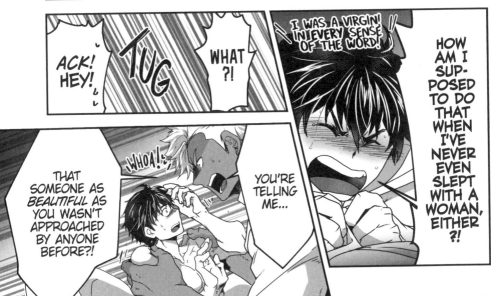

THAT SOMEONE AS *BEAUTIFUL* AS YOU WASN'T APPROACHED BY ANYONE BEFORE?!

WHOA!

YOU'RE TELLING ME...

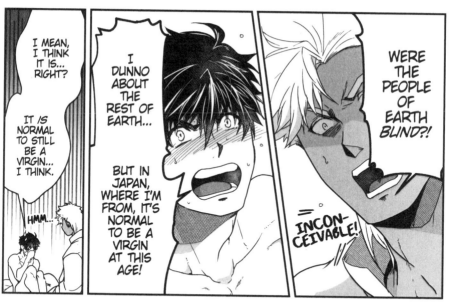

I MEAN, I THINK IT IS... RIGHT?

IT *IS* NORMAL TO STILL BE A VIRGIN... I THINK.

HMM...

I DUNNO ABOUT THE REST OF EARTH...

BUT IN JAPAN, WHERE I'M FROM, IT'S NORMAL TO BE A VIRGIN AT THIS AGE!

WERE THE PEOPLE OF EARTH *BLIND?!*

INCON-CEIVABLE!

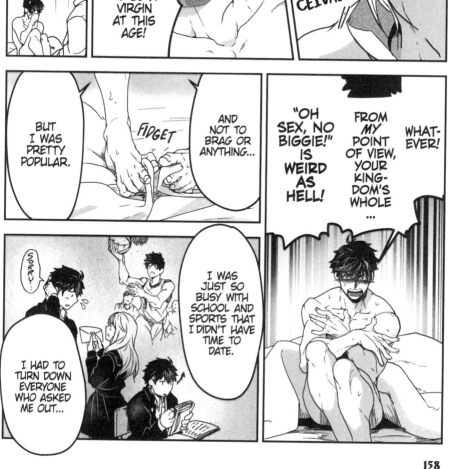

BUT I WAS PRETTY POPULAR.

FIDGET

AND NOT TO BRAG OR ANYTHING...

"OH SEX, NO BIGGIE!" IS WEIRD AS HELL!

FROM *MY* POINT OF VIEW, YOUR KING-DOM'S WHOLE ...

WHAT-EVER!

SORRY!...

I WAS JUST SO BUSY WITH SCHOOL AND SPORTS THAT I DIDN'T HAVE TIME TO DATE.

I HAD TO TURN DOWN EVERYONE WHO ASKED ME OUT...

KOUICHI.

SORRY...

THAT'S WHY I DON'T HAVE ANY EXPERIENCE OR ANY- THING...

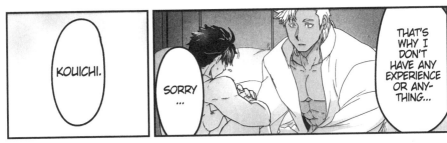

FOR THAT, I AM HONORED.

YOU GAVE ME THE PRIVILEGE OF SHARING YOUR FIRST EXPERIENCE.

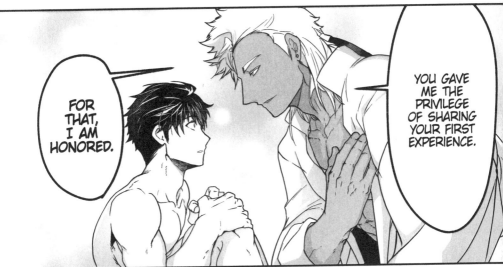

COULD YOU THINK OF ANYONE MORE SUITED TO BE YOUR FIRST?

WH-WHEN YOU PUT IT LIKE THAT, I DUNNO...

BUT...

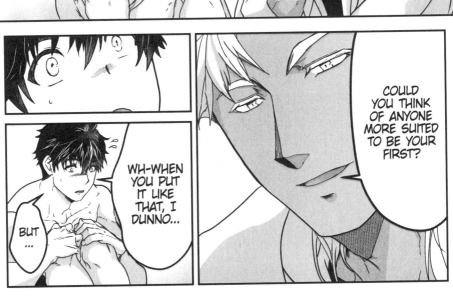

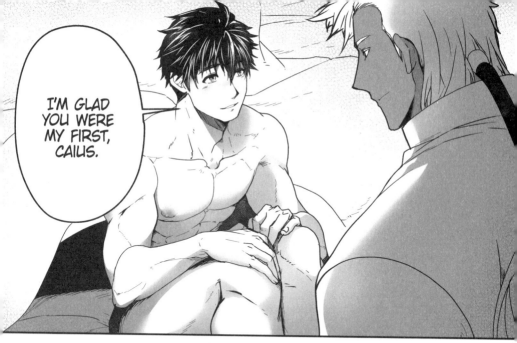

I'M GLAD YOU WERE MY FIRST, CAIUS.

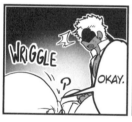

WRIGGLE

OKAY.

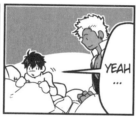

YEAH...

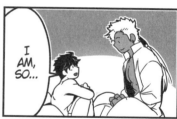

I AM, SO...

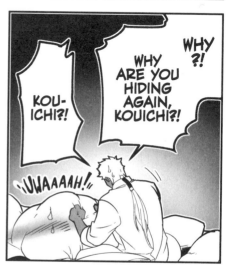

KOU-ICHI?!

WHY ARE YOU HIDING AGAIN, KOUICHI?!

WHY?!

UWAAAAH!!

- I-sama, my editor who was joined at my hip
- The editorial and production departments
- The colorist
- My assistants, Oomon-sama, Fujioka Yatsufusa-sama
- My friends and family who supported me all the way

And finally, my readers!

THANK YOU SO MUCH!

ITKZ

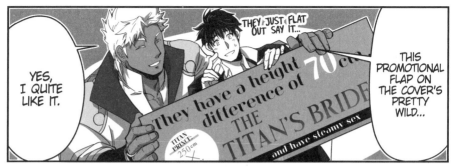

THIS PROMOTIONAL FLAP ON THE COVER'S PRETTY WILD...

YES, I QUITE LIKE IT.

THEY JUST FLAT OUT SAY IT...

They have a height difference of 70cm and have steamy sex

THE TITAN'S BRIDE

TITAN PRINCE: 250cm

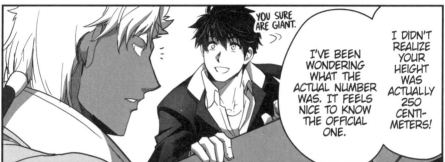

I DIDN'T REALIZE YOUR HEIGHT WAS ACTUALLY 250 CENTIMETERS!

I'VE BEEN WONDERING WHAT THE ACTUAL NUMBER WAS. IT FEELS NICE TO KNOW THE OFFICIAL ONE.

YOU SURE ARE GIANT.

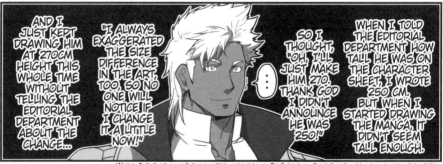

WHEN I TOLD THE EDITORIAL DEPARTMENT HOW TALL HE WAS ON THE CHARACTER SHEET, I WROTE 250 CM. BUT WHEN I STARTED DRAWING THE MANGA, IT DIDN'T SEEM TALL ENOUGH.

SO I THOUGHT, "OH, I'LL JUST MAKE HIM 270. THANK GOD I DIDN'T ANNOUNCE HE WAS 250!"

"I ALWAYS EXAGGERATED THE SIZE DIFFERENCE IN THE ART TOO, SO NO ONE WILL NOTICE IF I CHANGE IT A LITTLE NOW!"

AND I JUST KEPT DRAWING HIM AT 270CM HEIGHT THIS WHOLE TIME WITHOUT TELLING THE EDITORIAL DEPARTMENT ABOUT THE CHANGE...

...

※ TO BE EVEN MORE HONEST, I TOTALLY FORGOT I WROTE HE WAS 250 ON THE SHEET...

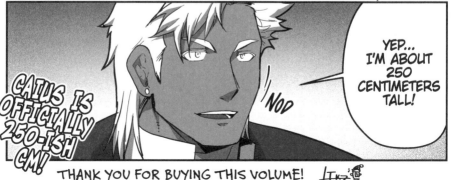

YEP... I'M ABOUT 250 CENTIMETERS TALL!

NOD

CAIUS IS OFFICIALLY 250-ISH CM!

THANK YOU FOR BUYING THIS VOLUME!

ALTERNATE UNIVERSE OF EUSTIL SUDDENLY MERGED WITH EARTH'S UNIVERSE,
AND NOW ITS RESIDENTS ARE ATTEMPT-ING TO COEXIST...
GOOD MORNING, CLASS.
A NEW STUDENT WILL BE JOINING YOU TODAY!
MY NAME IS CAIUS LAO VISTEIL, I HAIL FROM THE LAND OF GIANTS.
I HAVE TRAVELED HERE TO ENROLL AT THIS SCHOOL AT THE BEHEST OF A PROPHECY...
WHICH TELLS ME THIS IS WHERE I WILL FIND MY BRIDE.
......
NEW SERIES!
THE TITAN'S GROOM
THE NEW STUDENT IS A HEARTTHROB PRINCE WITH A HUGE DICK!
YOU CAN TAKE A SEAT NEXT TO MIZUKI-KUN THERE, IN THE BACK.
HOLD ON, THERE'S NO WAY THIS IS HAPPEN-ING!
THIS IS CRAZY!

THE TITAN'S BRIDE

VOLUME 2
COMING SOON!

THE
TITAN'S
BRIDE

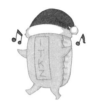

ITKZ
ITOKAZU

Birthday: 12/19
Blood Type: O

My first published
volume. I have
no words.

I hope you enjoy
this isekai
size-difference
BL story.

SEVEN SEAS ENTERTAINMENT PRESENTS

THE TITAN'S BRIDE

story and art by ITKZ   VOLUME ONE

TRANSLATION
Katrina Leonoudakis

LETTERING
Ray Steeves

PROOFREADER
Leighanna DeRouen

SENIOR COPY EDITOR
Dawn Davis

EDITOR
Kristiina Korpus

PREPRESS TECHNICIAN
Jules Valera

PRINT MANAGER
Rhiannon Rasmussen-Silverstein

PRODUCTION MANAGER
Lissa Pattillo

EDITOR-IN-CHIEF
Julie Davis

ASSOCIATE PUBLISHER
Adam Arnold

PUBLISHER
Jason DeAngelis

Kyojinzoku no hanayome volume 1
© ITKZ 2020
Originally published in Japan in 2020 by WWWave Corporation, Tokyo.
English translation rights arranged with WWWave Corporation, Tokyo,
through TOHAN CORPORATION, Tokyo.

Seven Seas press and purchase enquiries can be sent to Marketing Manager Lianne
Sentar at press@gomanga.com. Information regarding the distribution and purchase of
digital editions is available from Digital Manager CK Russell at digital@gomanga.com.

Seven Seas and the Seven Seas logo are trademarks of
Seven Seas Entertainment. All rights reserved.

ISBN: 978-1-63858-810-8
Printed in Canada
First Printing: October 2022
10 9 8 7 6 5 4 3 2 1

READING DIRECTIONS

This book reads from *right to left*,
Japanese style. If this is your first time
reading manga, you start reading from
the top right panel on each page and
take it from there. If you get lost, just
follow the numbered diagram here.
It may seem backwards at first,
but you'll get the hang of it! Have fun!!

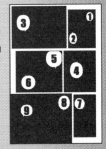